FORE   WORD

It has been in my mind quite for sometime after, I turned to the Lord God and found His grace that I should declare to the whole World, about the Grace of God Almighty.

Grace is the One Word, which is considered next to the Word of Love and it is just before the Word of Mercy in the dictionary of God.

I hope we all know that Love, Grace and Mercy, all these are the main three attributes of God Almighty and without any doubt 'Love' is the supreme above all other attributes of God towards the mankind.

The Bible (Word of God) declares about the 'Love' of God in this way;

"For God so loved the World that He gave His only begotten Son that whoever believes in Him should not

perish but have Everlasting Life"
(John3:16)

~~quickly~~

According to the Bible 'God is Love' and one of the Scripture of the Bible says about the "Love of God" in this way;

Love never fails; But where there are prophecies they will cease; Where there are tongues, they will be stilled and where there is knowledge, it will pass away.
(1 Corinthians 13: 8)

Now briefing about the 'Mercy of God', It will cease one day because God will not be 'Merciful' forever as He has to punish the wicked sinners after the final judgement for their Not repenting and not accepting the God. Mercy is a temporary attribute of God.

But "Grace of God" is not like the Mercy; It is like a guarantee or assurance from God, *when we repent for our sins and accept the Lord Jesus Christ as our only Saviour through our faith. Then surely we are on the safe side of the coin that is 'Redemption' and the other side of the coin is 'Destruction' for the unbelievers of God.*

So let us find the 'Grace of God' because the word of God declares in this way, "For by grace you have been saved through faith and that not of yourselves. It is the gift of God" (Ephesians 2: 8)

Here in this small book, I want to bring the hidden truth about the "Grace of God" which is the only option available now to the present and the last sinful generation of this earth; So as not only to escape the 'Wrath of God', but also be gifted with Eternal Life.

TABLE OF CONTENTS

Sl. No.   Name of the Chapter   Page No.

1. Redemption By Grace.   5

2. Nature of God.   11

3. God's Plan of Redemption.   20

4. Abraham The Father of Faith.   27

5. Job's Perseverance and Deliverance.   31

6. The First Elijah.   39

7. Deliverance of David- King of Israel.   57

8. Deliverance of Notorious Prisoner.   67

9. The Sufferings of Israel.   75

10. The Deliverance of Israel.   97

11. The Second Elijah.   119

12. An Examples for God's Grace.   128

13. Self Witness to the God's Grace.   142

14. Grace for the Last Generation.   158

1. REDEMPTION BY GRACE

But 'Noah' found grace in the eyes of the Lord.(Genesis 6: 8)

My beloved brothers and sisters!,

I call upon you to think seriously why but only 'Noah' found grace in the eyes of the Lord? When there were millions of families existed at that time on the earth!.

Here, I have an obligation towards my non-Christian brothers and sisters to explain that, who was 'Noah'? What was the situation at that time on the earth?.

And further when did the floods came and destroyed the whole earth? And why only Noah and his family were saved from these floods?

Well, to begin with Noah, he was the son of 'Lamech' a descendant of Adam and

Eve, the first couple on the earth who were created by God. And by the genealogy, Noah was of tenth generation beginning from Adam the first man Created in the image of God, by the Lord God Almighty.

What the Bible says about Noah? Let us go to the Scriptures, to the testament given to him.

"Noah was just man, perfect and blameless in his generations. Noah walked with God" (Genesis 6 : 9)

And Noah begot three sons; Sham, Ham and Japheth (Genesis 6:10 Now what was the situation on the earth at the time of Noah?

It should have been worse! I can surely say 'Worst Most' like these days of the earth.

How can you say? You may ask me! To prove, let us go to the days of Noah, mentioned in the Scriptures of the Bible.

Now it came to pass when men began to multiply on the face of the earth and daughters were born to them(Genesis 6: 1)

Note here that there was a population multiplication and increase like these days on the earth.

You may ask me that, how much increase could have been there out of the ten generations, That is beginning from Adam to Noah?

But please note also that the number of years, each of the first ten descendants of Adam lived!

Almost all of them lived more than Nine Hundred years except two of them. That is Enoch who lived 365 years and Lamech lived 777 years.

Now coming to the other situation on the earth during Noah's days, a small list of sins committed by men are enumerated below for easy understandings;-

Increase of Robberies and Lootings,

Adultery and Flourish of Homosexuality,

Too many Cheatings and Malpractices,

Rebellious and Disobedient Children,

Unrepentant & Remorseless generation,

Idolatry- A clear Blasphemy of God,

Lot of Violence and Murders on the earth,

Selfish and Greedy generation,

Increase of Unbelievers in God Almighty,

Increase in the Witchcraft.

The above mentioned sinful acts of human beings at that time of Noah are exactly fitting to the present generation(I hope you understand now) caused God to bring an end by the floods on that sinful generation.

Now only Noah, and his wife, then his three sons and three daughters- in law totalling 8 (eight) in numbers were saved from these floods.

All these eight people were saved only because of the Noah's Righteousness through his faith in God Almighty.

When the whole generation of the earth at that time was fully corrupted, Noah was perfect and blameless and righteous man in the eyes of the Lord and that is what the Bible says about him.

Is it not amazing? Yes!, and I very much doubt that there will be another Noah or anyone like him in these last days of this earth.

But of course!, there will be many in millions who will be saved through their faith in the Lord Jesus Christ.

Because the Word of God by the prophet Joel 2:32 of the Bible says about the Redemption of people in the last days of this earth;

And it shall come to pass that whoever calls on the name of the Lord shall be saved (delivered from going to hell) (Joel 2: 32)

What does it mean? It does not mean that anyone calling on the Lord Jesus Christ without repenting for their sins!

It means believing that Jesus Christ is the only Lord God and Savior and further putting all their faith in Him for their Redemption which is called Salvation.

_____

2. NATURE OF GOD

In the beginning God created the heavens and the earth. (Genesis 1:1)

Hear 'O' Israel, the Lord our God, the Lord is one!. (Deuteronomy 6: 4)

Dear my brothers and sisters! What do you grasp out of the above two Scriptures of the Bible?

Is it not one thing? That there is only one God and He only created the heavens and the earth!.

In fact it is the absolute truth; Now to make it more clear let us go to another Scripture from the Bible, which says;

Is God, the God of Jews only? Is He not also the God of Gentiles? Yes, of the Gentiles also!.(Romans 3: 29)

I believe that this Scripture of Bible, clears the doubt (if any)of my Gentile brothers and sisters, that there is only one God and He is the Creator of all, Savior of all and Sanctifier of all. Amen.

Here I, call upon my brothers and sisters of Israel to forgive me! I know that You are very jealous for the Lord (i.e. Jehovah) but I am sad only because you could not recognise your own 'Messiah', Jesus Christ the Lord!

Now let us see, what God has proclaimed about Himself to Moses, His servant when He passed in front of Moses.

And the Lord God passed before him (Moses) and proclaimed, "The Lord God, Merciful and Gracious, Long suffering and abounding in Goodness and truth. (Exodus 34: 6)

So the Lord God is Merciful, meaning that He is ready to forgive the sins of those who repent and accept Him as their God and Savior.

Here I want to quote two Important Scriptures of the Bible in which God says, "For I desire Mercy and not Sacrifice" (Hosea 6: 6)

Let the wicked forsake his way; And the evil man his thoughts; Let him turn to the Lord and He will have mercy on him and to our God, for He will freely pardon (Isaiah 55: 7)

What we learn from the above two Scriptures is, that God expects us to repent for our sins and seek Him faithfully, so that He can show us Mercy.

He also does not want the people to seek Him by their sacrifices of animals which are no use at all, after Jesus Christ the Lord shed His innocent and Godly blood on the Cross.

Now coming to explain about the Gracefulness of God, I believe that I am the right person to explain it because I was the worst most sinner on the earth; yet I am living only by the "Grace of God" which has come to me through our Lord Jesus Christ.

At one stage of my life, I thought that I have committed all sins except the Murder. But of late now, the Holy Spirit revealed to me that I was also murderer, because I have made my wife to undergo abortions, where I have killed innocent babies in the womb itself.

Here I am not encouraging you to sin more, so that more grace may come upon you, but to repent for your sins and believe the Lord Jesus Christ, for He is the only way to receive God's grace. Amen.

Now coming to explain another nature of God that is 'Long suffering' or we can say in simple language the "Patience of God".

You should understand and realise in your own life, how many times you were let go free by God for your abominable sins and wickedness committed against not only God but also against fellow human beings.

Honestly if you can count them, they will surpass the good things you have done in your life. Now some one (unbeliever) may boost saying that "I am over sixty years old and I can't count or even remember the sins, which I have committed; Yet I am living a healthy and prosperous life.

But to that unbelieving brother, I declare today that ' God is patiently' waiting for you all these sixty years, thinking that you may repent soon, that is before the day of death comes to you.

Here I want to quote one of the important Scripture of the Bible which says,

"Do I take any pleasure in death of the wicked? Declares the Sovereign Lord. Rather, am I not pleased when they turn from their ways and live".(Ezekiel 18: 23)

So, please do not test the patience of God and the moment when you come to know about the "Living and Just full God" that is the time for your repentance and acceptance by His grace.

Explaining other two natures of God, that He is abounding in Goodness and Truth; Here I want to take the example of the Lord Jesus Christ who was God in the flesh for nearly thirty three and half (33 ½) years.

Firstly He preached "Good News about the Heavenly Kingdom" which is likely to come soon on this earth.

Secondly, when He has seen the sufferings of the people, He had compassion on them.

Then by His Almighty power, He has opened eyes of the blind and healed the Deaf and Dumb, so they can see, hear and speak well. He also healed the lame, so they walked as normal people.

He has cast out evil spirits from the afflicted people; He also performed many miracles by which, wiped out tears of many suffering from various diseases. Over and above He has raised the dead by proving that He has the power of God.

In spite of all these good works of Him, that is His abounding goodness, He has been crucified on the Cross. Even when He was about to die on the Cross, He forgave the people who crucified Him. What more than can be said of Him? Is it not proving that He is abounding in Goodness?

Surely without any doubt!

Now telling about the Truth, that is the another nature of God; Let us go to the Scriptures of the Bible which says,

"But the Lord is true God; He is the living God and the eternal King (Jeremiah 10: 10)

"Declaring the end from the beginning; And from ancient times, things that are not yet come saying My counsel shall stand and I will do all My pleasure"(Isaiah46:10)

Now both of these two Scriptures are from Old Testament of the Bible, that is before the Christ Era and they tell us that there is One Eternal God and He is true in fulfilling His Word.

These Scriptures of God also tell us that, what will be the end, even from the be ginning to the end time events which were foretold by Him through His prophets.

Now a day's things are happening exactly what was prophesied about four thousand years ago and what was prophesied by the Lord Jesus Christ, two thousand years before.

In the New Testament of the Bible, Lord Jesus Christ, says about Himself,

"I am the Way and the Truth and the Life" (John 14: 6)

If Jesus Christ, the Lord is not the Truth, who then can be?

Can anyone show a book except the Bible where its prophecies are coming into deeds, exactly as foretold from the beginning to even today?

What does it mean? It means "Only God is Faithful" and "Only the "Bible is Truthful" word of God that all these good natures originate only from Him.

3. GOD'S PLAN OF REDEMPTION

My brothers and sisters! What do you understand by the word of Redemption?

According to the Oxford Dictionary, Redeem (verb) or Redemption (noun) meaning to compensate for the faults or save from the sin. There is also a meaning-Fulfilling promise of Redemption.

What is the necessity for Redemption?, Unless something very important has been snatched from us! Or else something highly valuable belongs to us has been wrongly mortgaged.

Yes!, Adam and Eve, our first parents were cheated by the 'Lucifer' who is called Satan by his seduction and trickery!; So they forfeited their Immortality which was bestowed by their Creator, the Lord God Almighty.

Satan has seduced the Eve, the wife of Adam and indirectly caused Adam to disobey the simple commandment of God, thereby brought Death to Adam and Eve and to everyone after them, that is to us, since we are all the descendants of Adam and Eve.

There is a Scripture from the Bible, which explains about Redemption better way,

"Therefore, just as sin entered the world through one man(Adam) and death, through sin and in this way death came to all men because all sinned"(Romans 5: 12)

Therefore it was necessary to redeem the fallen man from the sin, so as to save him from the death.

But who can redeem the fallen man?

Is it possible by another man who is also a sinner? Impossible! No chance at all!

Now To explain this, in simple and dramatic way, let us take an example of proceedings of a Judicial Court of this earth.

Suppose, one of my brother is arrested by police for some criminal act and then after interrogation, produced before a Magistrate in his Judicial Court.

And if I wanted to bring my brother "Out on Bail", Do you know what the Judge of this Judicial Court will ask me first?

"Is there any criminal case pending against you? Or have you ever been convicted by any other court earlier?

In my reply, If I say to the Judge, "Yes sir, I have been convicted or say that there is a Criminal case pending against me";

Do you know, what will be the Judge's reaction?

My sweet brother and sister, the Judge will rebuke me and say,

"You are already accused and convicted! How dare then, you come to bail out your accused brother?"

He will also say, 'Therefore go and come up with a man who is not accused or not committed any crime!, Then I will grant a bail to your accused brother"

So like in this manner, the Judge will rebuke me!, because I have a criminal case pending against me in the Judicial court.

If this is the condition of an earthly court, How anyone who has inherited sin right from his birth and then goes on sinning in his life period, can be bailed out from the spiritual death?

So, please think it over my brothers and sisters that no man can be bailed out from his spiritual death!

That is why, God alone is holy, innocent and righteous, who came into the world in the name of Jesus Christ and paid ransom for our sins on the Cross when He died for us, so as to set us free from the sin and then later from the spiritual death. Praise the Lord!

In the Old Testament there is an event in the history of Israel which can be taken as an example or shadow for the Redemption or Salvation of the mankind.

Out of four hundred(400) years of Israel's history in the land of Egypt, Israelis were free people (not under slavery) for seventy (70) years in the beginning, as Joseph(one of the twelve sons of Jacob) was governor of Egypt at that time

But after the death of Joseph, Israelites were enslaved for about three hundred and thirty (330) years by Egyptians and

Pharaohs, kings of Egypt and were longing to come out of their slavery.

Now the Lord God, instructed Moses to ensure that all Israelites to slaughter a male lamb without blemish or any defect, each one according to the need of the family and sprinkle its blood on the door post of their houses without fail.

So all the Israelites obeyed the instruction of Moses, the Man of God, and sprinkled the blood of the lambs on the door posts of their houses and eaten the roasted meat of the lambs, exactly in the they were instructed.

Then God has sent His angels who came down with His wrath and put to death all Egyptian's first born males and not touched any Israelites, when the angels saw the blood on the door posts of their houses.

So all the Israelites in Egypt were delivered from their slavery and were let go free by God's grace.

Same way, God's plan for the salvation of the people of this earth was to send His Only begotten Son, having His name to shed His innocent blood on the Cross and die as atonement Lamb for the sinners of the world.

So Jesus Christ, God in the flesh came and shed His innocent blood on the Cross and died for our sins and rose to life on the third (3rd) day to prove that we can also overcome the death through our faith in Him.

Since it was impossible by any man to redeem the sinful mankind, Jesus Christ, the Lord came to free the man from the sin and the curse of the death, brought by Satan, the enemy of God and His people.

4. ABRAHAM - THE FATHER OF FAITH

And he (Abraham) believed in the Lord and the Lord accounted to him for Righteousness (Genesis 15: 6)

What a wonderful and truthful statement! That is about the patriarch Abraham by the word of God. In fact this commendation from God is even before Abraham was circumcised in the flesh.

Let us examine how this commendation has come from God to Abraham? And what was the situation?

Now Abraham was ninety years old and his wife Sarah was eighty years old and they were childless; Abraham was thinking that after him, one of his servants may become his heir.It was about 3 p.m. in the afternoon; The Lord God appeared to Abraham and instructed to prepare evening sacrifice and by the time Abraham prepared, it was already dark and he was in great fear.

Now the Lord God appeared again in the form of fire, walked through the sacrifice of Abraham as an acceptance of him.

Then the Lord God promised Abraham that there will be descendants from his own body and he need not to worry, thinking "who will be his heir after him.

Then the Lord brought Abraham outside and said, "Look now towards heaven and count the stars if you are able to number them." And He said to him, "So shall your descendants be" (Genesis 15: 5)

At that very moment Abraham believed the Lord God that He is able to give to him child even in his old age through Sarah his wife, who has crossed the age of child bearing.   Praise the Lord!

Now the Lord God has fulfilled His promise by giving Abraham a son Isaac through Sarah his wife, when he was hundred years and Sarah ninety years old respectively.

Please note here that not out of mercy, God has given a son to Abraham, but because of the faith that Abraham had in God Almighty.

Abraham did not linger in faith, though God has promised him, when he was seventy five years of age, that Lord will make him a great nation!, But blessed him with the son Isaac at the age of hundred years.

God has tested the Abraham's faith, precisely his patience for about twenty five years and then fulfilled His promise of giving Abraham, Isaac the son of His promise.Here also Abraham did not linger in his obedience to the Lord besides his faith in the Lord God Almighty!

Then Abraham took his only son Isaac to the Mount Moriah and there laid his son on the alter and was about to slay him by a sword to sacrify to the Lord.

But the Lord God stopped him, doing that and commended Abraham's faith and obedience, thereby received the blessings of the Lord in this way;

In blessing I will bless you and in multiplying I will multiply your descen dants as the stars of the heaven and as the sand which is on the seashore; and your descendants shall posses the gate of their enemies.(Genesis 22:17)

In your Seed (Jesus Christ) all the nations of the earth shall be blessed, because you have obeyed My voice.(Genesis 22:18)

So these are the reasons, why Abraham is being called "The Father of Faith" even today. Praise the Lord

5.JOB'S PERSEVERANCE AND DELIVERANCE

My dear brothers and sisters!
There was a man called 'Job' who lived in the land of 'UZ', that was in present Syria about one thousand and five hundred years before the Christ Era.(B.C.)

Now this man owned seven thousand sheep, three thousand camels, and five hundred yoke of oxen and five hundred donkeys besides large number of servants.

He had seven sons and three daughters all of them grown up adults, who is to celebrate parties at the weekends in their houses turn wise, according to their numbers.

Now Job was righteous man, he feared God and used to sanctify his sons and daughters by fasting himself to the Lord and offer burnt sacrifices to God at the end of fasting.

Now, let us go to the event which took place in the heaven during those good times of Job's life on the earth.

There was a day when angels of God came to present themselves, before the Lord and Satan also came among them.

Then the Lord said to Satan, "Have you considered My servant Job that there is no one like him on the earth, a blameless and upright man, one who fears God and shun evil? (Job 1: 8)

So, Satan answered the Lord and said, "Does Job fears God for nothing? (Job 1: 9)

Have you not made a edge around him, around his household and around all that he has, on every side? You have blessed the work of his hands and his possessions have increased in the land.(Job 1 : 10)

"But now stretch out Your hand and touch all that he has and he will surely curse You to Your face" (Job 1:11)

"And the Lord said to Satan, "Behold all that he has is in your hands, only do not lay a hand on his person" So, the Satan went out from the presence of the Lord. (Job 1:12)

Now my brothers and sisters, you know what conversation took place in the heaven regarding the Job the servant of the Lord!

Since Lord God has given power to Satan, to take away all things belongs to Job; Satan acted swiftly to destroy everything that belongs to him.

Job's three thousand camels were taken away by bandits (Chaldeans) who came from Iraq and killed all his servants except one who were in the fields.

Then all his seven thousand sheep along with shepherds were completely destroyed by a fire which came from above; only one shepherd was spared to inform this matter to his master Job.

Then Job's five hundred yokes of oxen and five hundred donkeys were taken away by Sabeans, from Sheba after killing Job's herdsmen. Only one man was left to inform the matter to the Job.

Lastly all his seven sons and three daughters were killed when there was a party at the house of his eldest son. The building in which they gathered together has collapsed and every one was killed except one of his servant who informed Job about the incident.

What a disaster! Just see how fast the Satan, the Devil acted against the Job! Just imagine if we were in the place of Job, what could have we done?

Surely we would have cursed God!

Let us see what Job did when he lost everything that includes all his sons and daughters who died in one day?

Then Job arose, tore his robe and shaved his head and he fell to the ground and worshiped the Lord. (Job 1:20)

And he said," Naked I came from my mother's womb and naked shall I return there. The Lord gave and the Lord has taken away; "Blessed be the name of the Lord. (Job 1: 21)

Now there was another day, once again Satan went along with angels into the presence of God in the heaven and the Lord God asked him;

"Have you considered My servant Job that there is none like him on the earth; A blameless and upright man, one who fears God and shuns evil. And still he holds fast

to his integrity, although you incited Me against him to destroy him without cause. (Job 2: 3)

Satan replied, "Skin for skin, Yes, man will give everything he has for his life. Now lay your hand on his bone and flesh, he will surely curse You to Your face." (Job 2: 4-5)

Then the Lord said to Satan, "Behold he is in your hand, you should not take his life." So, Satan came out from the presence of the Lord and struck the Job with painful boils from the soles of his feet to the scalp of his head.

Then his wife said to him, "Do you still hold fast to your integrity? Curse God and die!" (Job 2: 9)

But Job rebuked his wife telling her," Shall we accept only good from the Lord and not any adversity

Even to the end Job did not curse Lord God for all his sufferings!.

Then came his three friends to see him; And they saw Job sitting outside of his house on the heap of ashes and scraping his wounds with a piece of pot shred.

Instead of consoling or comforting the Job, with their soothing words, his friends started accusing him falsely without any knowledge of his earlier life.

So, they advised Job to repent for his youthful sins and wickedness, so that God may reduce his sufferings.

Then Job rebuked his friends severely, telling them that he is not inferior to them either in the knowledge or wisdom or even in the righteousness.

He also rebuked them for accusing him falsely without any knowledge and *justification and also for not consoling him in his misery.*

In his integrity and faith in the Lord, Job declared to his friends telling them, "Though God may slay me, Yet I will trust in Him.(Job 13 : 15)

So, my brothers and sisters, let us endeavour and pray to the God for His Grace, through our acts of faith in the Lord God Almighty.

---

6. THE FIRST ELIJAH

What do you mean by the First Elijah?, You may ask me!

Yes, my brothers and sisters, It means there are more than One Elijah!; But we are going to see here, what the First Elijah has done in his life time.

Now before going to the life period of Elijah, let us find the meaning for the name Elijah.

In Hebrew language, Elijah means "Jehovah is my God"

Now most of the Israelites, in olden days had their names origination from the titles of God or related to His holy name.

Elijah, the prophet lived during the period of the kings in the history of Israel, that is during the periods of Omri, Ahab and

Ahaziah, kings of Israel and Asa and Jehoshaphat kings of Judah who ruled from Samaria and Jerusalem respectively.

It seems Elijah was in his forties of his age, when he was taken up alive into the heaven in the Chariot of fire and most probably has done Lord's ministry for about 15 years.

Now let us see what he has done in the name of the Lord and why he has to come back second or even third time that is at the end of the earth.

Elijah was a great Prophet of God came from Gilead, the other side of Jordan River that is presently in Jordan nation. He prophesied more during the time of Ahab the king of Israel.

Now let us see, what was the condition of Israel during the time of Ahab, the king of Israel?

Idolatry!Idolatry! And Idolatry everywhere!

Most of the Israelites, under the king of Ahab's rule rebelled against the Lord God by worshiping the abominable Idols.

There were two culprits who caused the Israelites to forsake the Lord their God and worship the detestable Idols.

The first culprit was Omri, the father of Ahab king of Israel. When Omri became the king of Israel, he did evil by bringing Idol worship into the land of Israel.

Now let us see what the Scriptures say about him?

"Omri did evil in the eyes of the Lord and did worse than all who were before him"(1 Kings 16 : 25)

For he walked in all the ways of 'Jeroboam' son of Nabat and in his sin by which he had made Israel to sin, provoking the Lord God of Israel to anger with their Idols. (1 Kings 16: 26)

King Omri ruled the Israel for twelve years and when he died, his son Ahab not only inherited the Kingdom but also the policy of Idol worship from his father.

Now coming to the second culprit, who brought Idol worship, a custom of pagans into Israel, was none other than the wife of Ahab, whose name was "Jezebel", She was a daughter of Ethbaal a pagan king of Sidon.

It is because of her pagan's beliefs and customs she brought the Idols of Baal and Asherah, the gods of Siderites' and Canaanites into Israel.

As a queen of Israel with authority of her husband Ahab the king, she has installed Idols of Baal and Asherah poles in every street corner of villages and cities of Israel.

Further she also ordained four hundred and fifty prophets of Baal and four hundred priests of Asherah the pagan gods to serve them.

So this was the situation, that is Idolatry everywhere!, during the rule of Ahab and his pagan wife Jezebel.

Now at this juncture "The First Elijah" sent by God came to Ahab, the king of Israel and rebuked him severely for the abominable Idol worship.

Let us go to the Scriptures of the Bible in this regard;

Elijah the Tishbite of the inhabitants of Gilead said to Ahab, "As the Lord God of Israel lives, before whom I stand, there shall not be dew or rain, these years except atmyword"(1Kings17:1)
What a powerful and daring prophecy! That is also by an unknown person to Ahab

First of all, King Ahab does not know who the Elijah was, since he has seen him first time.

Then when he was confronted suddenly, by Elijah with his powerful prophecy, he became speechless. Further Ahab wondered that who can be this man Elijah?, since all the prophets of the Lord were killed by his wife Jezebel.

Now by the time, Ahab came to his senses, Elijah the prophet has left him already.

From that time onwards under the curse of the prophet Elijah, the whole land of Israel has suffered "Draught", No rain or dew fallen on the land of Israel and surrounding countries.

Now water resources like brooks, ponds, lakes and rivers started drying up causing great famine all over Israel and surrounding countries as there was no rain.

But Ahab did not bother about his people sufferings due to this draught; where as he has instructed his servant Obadiah to find out green pastures for his horses and mules, so they may not perish.

Now Ahab the king started searching Elijah the prophet, everywhere including in the surrounding countries, to punish him for his curse.

So all the people of Israel came to know about the Elijah, the prophet and his curse on the land which lasted about 3 ½ years.

Now Elijah remained in Israel for about six months, living by the side of fresh water brook. But when the brook dried, he went to Zerephath, a village in Sidon to live in a house of a widow, as per the word of God.

Here Elijah stayed until the end of the draught period and Ahab the king of Israel could not locate him during this period.

Elijah the prophet performed couple of miracles in the house of the widow, where he stayed and let us see what he has done there?

When Elijah came to Zerephath and met the widow to whom he was sent by God, he asked her to bring him little bread and water.

But she said to him, "Sir, I have only handful of flour and little oil in my house by which I am going to make bread for me and my son, then eat and die."

After listening her anguishing words, Elijah said to the widow;

Do not fear, go and do as you have said, but make me a small cake from it first and bring it to me; And afterward make some for you and your son. (1 King 17:13)

"For thus says the Lord God of Israel; The bin of flour shall not be used up nor shall

the jar of oil run dry until the day the Lord sends rain on the earth.(1 King 17 : 14)

So, she went and did according to the word of Elijah the prophet and the result was, her son her household all ate until the draught ended.

Now let us come to the second miracle, Elijah the prophet performed with the power of the Lord at the same house of the widow where he stayed.

After sometime the widow's son became seriously ill and died in his sickness.

Then the widow stricken by grief said to Elijah, "What have I to do with you 'O' man of God. Have you come to bring my sin to remembrance and to kill my son" (1 King 17: 18)

Immediately Elijah took her son's body and went to his upper room and laid him on his bed and stretched himself out on the boy three times and cried out to the Lord and said;

'O' Lord my God, "I pray let this child's life come back to him.(1 King 17: 21)

Then the Lord heard the voice of Elijah and the soul of the child came back to him and he revived.(1 King 17: 22)

When the widow saw her son came alive, she exclaimed and said to Elijah, Now by this I know that you are a man of a God! And the word of the Lord in your mouth is the truth.(1King 17: 24)

Elijah the prophet, stayed there for about three years and then the word of the Lord came to him saying, "Now arise and go to the Ahab, king of Israel and proclaim that the Lord is going to send rain on the earth.

So, as per the word of the Lord, Elijah went to Ahab who was at Samaria in Israel.

When Ahab saw Elijah after 3 ½ years, he said to him;

Is not you, 'O' trouble of Israel?, Why did you come here again?

Elijah shot back and said, "I have not troubled Israel, but you and your father's house have!. In that you have forsaken the Lord's commandments and followed Baal and Asherah the false gods.

Now therefore send and gather and all Israel to me on the mount Carmel, the four hundred fifty prophets of Baal and four hundred priests of Asherah, who eat at Jezebel's(1 kings 18 : 18)

So, Ahab the king of Israel sent for all people and gathered them along with all priests and prophets of pagan gods together on the Mount Carmel.

Now, Elijah said to the Israelites gathered to him on Mount Carmel, How long will you falter between two opinions; If the Lord is God fallow Him! But if the Baal follow him and all kept quite.

Then Elijah said to them, I am alone left, the only prophet of the Lord and you see here four hundred fifty prophets of Baal.

Let the king give us two bulls; and let the prophets of Baal choose one bull for themselves, cut it in pieces and lay it on the wood, but put no fire under it.

Then let the prophets of Baal call on their god and I will call on the name of the Lord. The God who answers by fire, He is God. So all the people answered and said, It is well spoken. (1 King 18 : 24)

So, the prophets of Baal prepared and laid the pieces of the cut bull, on their alter and called on their gods from morning till afternoon.

They cried aloud and cut themselves as was their custom, with the knives and lances until blood oozed out of them. But nothing has happened, and no god answered them by fire to burn their sacrifice.

So, after four hours (10 am to 2pm) useless rituals and prophesies by the prophets of Baal, Elijah the prophet of the Lord taken over.

Firstly, he prepared the alter for the sacrifice, doing so, he took twelve stones commemorating each one for twelve tribes of Israel in the name of the Lord. Then he dug a trench around the altar, large enough to hold about six hundred litres of water.

Then Elijah put the wood in order and cut the bull in pieces and laid it on the wood and asked them to fill the four water pots with water and pour it on the sacrifice.

They did so, but Elijah made them to pour water second and third time with same quantity of water on the sacrifice.

Now, water ran into the trench around the altar and the trench was filled. The whole wood on the altar also was wet. The people of Israel watched Elijah breathlessly all these things and now the time was about 3 pm in the afternoon.

Elijah stood amidst of the people, near to the altar, lifted up his hands and head towards the heaven and prayed saying;

"O" Lord God of Abraham, Isaac and Jacob, let it be known today that You are God and that I am Your servant and that I have done all these things at Your word.

Hear me 'O' Lord, hear me, that this people may know that You are the Lord God and You have turned their hearts back to You again.(1 Kings 18 : 37)

Then the fire of the Lord fell and consumed the burnt sacrifice and the wood and the stones and the dust and it also licked up the water that was in the trench.

Now, when all the people of Israel saw it they fell on their faces to the ground and said, "The Lord, He is God! The Lord, He is God!"

Elijah said to the people, "Seize the prophets of Baal!, Do not let one of them escape!. So they seized them and Elijah brought them down to the Kishon Valley and there executed all of them.

Then to mention here, the last but not the least action of the 'First Elijah" during his lifetime was, destroying his enemies by bringing fire from the heaven.

After the death of Ahab, king of Israel, his son Ahazia reigned in his place. When Ahazia was injured, he sent some of his men to enquire Baalzerub, the god of Ekron, asking whether he will recover or not.

But Elijah the prophet, sent these men back to Ahazia, before they could go and enquire the pagan god, telling them that king Ahazia will die and not recover from his injury.

When Ahazia came to know the comments of Elijah, he sent fifty of his soldiers with a captain to arrest Elijah and bring him to Samaria so as to prosecute him.

But Elijah, sitting on top of the hill prayed to the Lord and fire came from heaven and destroyed all of them who came to arrest him.

Angered by the incident king Ahazia sent another batch of fifty soldiers with a captain to arrest Elijah. They also faced the same fate of the first batch of the soldiers.

Then Ahazia, the king of Israel became so furious that he sent again for the last time a captain with fifty soldiers to arrest the Elijah and drag him down to Samaria.

This time, the captain who led the fifty soldiers was wise; He came to the Elijah, fell on his face before him and pleaded to forgive him and the soldiers as they are only obeying the command of the king.

So, Elijah forgave them and went down with the captain and the soldiers to face Ahazia at Samaria. And when he came to Ahazia the king, the prophet Elijah said;

"Thus says the Lord, because you sent messengers to enquire, Baal Zeus, the god of Ekron, "Is it because there is no God in Israel to enquire of His word? Therefore, you shall not come down from the bed to which you have gone up; but you shall die (2 kings 1:16)

So the king Ahazia died according to the word of God by the mouth of Elijah the prophet who lived during the days of kings of Israel.

Now concluding this chapter here, by stating that the First Elijah was empowered;

To shut up the heaven without rain to devastate the earth.

To bring down fire from the heaven to destroy his enemies.

To increase the provisions of the desperate widow of Zerephath in Sidon.

To raise the dead to life of the son of same widow of Zerephath in Sidon.

_____ -

7. DELIVERANCE OF DAVID KING OF ISRAEL

Beloved my brothers and sisters, I want to reveal to you, how Grace of God, came upon the king David who has ruled Israel for more than forty years.

Who was the king David?

David was not born in the king's family!, His father Jesse a descendant of Judah, was a farmer and shepherd. David's father owned lands and flocks of sheep.

Young David, about fifteen years old, after his formal education was sent by his father Jesse to tend his sheep in the open fields.

So, David was a Shepherd primarily by his profession. The young David was handsome and courageous, that is bold enough, that one day he has killed a young lion which has come to attack his flocks while he was tending them in the open fields.

Well, then the Lord changed his life into the great warrior of Israel, when he single handily went and killed 'Goliath' the Philistian (who was over 9 feet) by his famous sling shot, when Saul was the king over Israel.

David became very famous in the army of Israel for his valiant deeds that even Saul the king became jealous of him.

There was a song among young women of Israel, at that time about young David singing, "Saul has slain his thousands; And David has ten thousands!"

When Saul and his son Jonathan both were killed by Philistians in the war, Israel was divided into two kingdoms and David became king over Judah while Isbosheth, another son of Saul was made king over Israel.

Then after few years when Isbosheth, king of Israel was killed by two of his own captains, David became the king over undivided and united Israel.

After becoming the king over all Israel, David fought many battles and won every one of them.

Now coming to the one big act of the king David, which was branded as wickedness in the sight of God and his people of Israel.

Here is the incident!, During one of the spring time of the year, when the kings usually go to the war, king David stayed back in his palace and sent 'Joab' his commander to fight the battle with Ammonites at Rabbah.

He was idle at his place and to pass the time, one evening that is before sunset

, he walked on the terrace of his palace.

At that time David saw a woman bathing in her topless makeshift bathroom of her house, which was adjacent to the palace.

Now the woman was very young and beautiful to behold and the king David immediately sent and enquired about the woman.

He was told that her name was "Bathsheba" and she was the wife of "Uriah", a soldier fighting his battle under the command of Joab at that time.

Then he sent for her, when she came, he lay with her for she was cleansed from her impurity and in the morning, king David has sent her back to her house.

She conceived immediately and sent a word about this to the king David. Then David sent a messenger to Joab saying, "Send me Uriah the soldier immediately.

And Joab his commander promptly sent Uriah to the king David.

When Uriah had come to him, David enquired about the battle and then said to him; "Go down to your house and relax as you are weary of the battle."

But Uriah did not go to his house, where as slept in that night at the servant quarters of the king. When the king learned about this in the morning, he called Uriah and said, "Why didn't you go to your house?

Then Uriah replied, "When my commander Joab and fellow soldiers are fighting the battle, Shall I go to my house to eat and drink and lay with my wife? As you live 'O' king, I will not do such thing!

The following night also Uriah did not go to his house, where as ate and slept at the servant quarters of the king David.

Next day morning, David wrote letter to Joab saying, "Set Uriah in the forefront of the hottest battle line and then retreat from him that he may be stuck down and die"

He sealed the letter and sent it, by the very hands of Uriah to hand over to his commander Joab. As innocent man not knowing his fate, Uriah carried the letter and gave it to Joab.

Joab the commander understood quickly and did the same as the king David instructed in his letter.

Ultimately as per the wicked plan of the king David, Uriah the husband of "Bathsheba" died in the hottest battle front.

When the death of Uriah was confirmed by the messenger sent by Joab, king David sent back to Joab saying, "Do not let this *thing displease you, for the sword devours one as well as the other"*

Later David brought "Bathsheba" into his palace and took her as his wife.

Now this is the true story of the king David and his only wickedness committed in his whole life.

At this period of time, God has sent His prophet 'Nathan' to David telling him a story, by which Lord God, purposed to bring king David to severe repentance.

Now let us see what was the story told by Nathan, the prophet of God to the king David?

There were two men lived in the city; one was rich and the other poor. The rich man had exceedingly many flocks of sheep and herds of cattle.

But the poor man had only 'One ewe lamb' which he bought and nourished. It ate of his food and drank from his cup and lay in his bosom. It was like a daughter to him.

Then a guest came to the rich man, who had many flocks of sheep. Instead of taking one of his sheep from his flocks to prepare for the guest, rich man went and took the poor man's only ewe lamb and prepared it for his guest.

Now after listening the story, king David became furious with anger and said to Nathan the prophet, " As the Lord lives, the man who has done this shall surely die".

Then Nathan said to David, "You are the man!"Thus says the Lord God of Israel, "I anointed you king over Israel and I delivered you from the hand of Saul" (Refer 2Samuel 12:5-7)

Why have you despised the commandment of the Lord to do evil in His sight? You have killed Uriah the Hittite with the sword. You have taken his wife to be his wife and have killed him with sword of people of Ammon. (2 Samuel 12:9)

So, David said to Nathan, "I have sinned against the Lord", And Nathan said to David, the Lord also put away your sin, and you shall not die. (2 Samuel 12:13)

My brothers and sisters!
You believe it or not, there is no one in human beings like king David, who has repented in his whole life!
He wept and wept and cried for his wickedness!, He pleaded guilty and prayed for the Mercy and Grace from the Lord God Almighty.

As a result king David sung and written more than a hundred of Psalms, calling us to repent for our sins and wickedness.

All his Psalms were sung and written by him, when he was filled with 'Holy Spirit' revealing the promises of God, in form of Prophecies, especially about Messiah's (Christ) coming, suffering and death on the Cross for our deliverance.

So my brothers and sisters!,

Let us cry and pray to the Lord to give us, the heart of David for our repentance, then surely we will find Grace of God saving us from all our visible and invisible enemies. Amen.   Praise the Lord!

———————————————————-

8.DELIVERANCE OF NOTORIOUS PRISONER

Now let us come to the New Testament of Bible, where a notorious Prisoner, condemned to death and how he was delivered from his punishment of death, just in time by the grace of God.

The man was none other than "Barabbas", the notorious prisoner mentioned in the Scriptures of the Bible written by Mathew 27:15-26, and Mark 15: 6-15.

Now this man Barabbas was a leader of the rebellious movement and he with two of his accomplice, were condemned to death, for they committed murders and robberies in their rebellion against the Roman government at that time in Israel.

The following Scriptures of the Bible will enlighten us in this regard, "And there was one named 'Barabbas' who was chained.

with his fellow rebels and they had com mitted murder in the rebellion(Mark15:7)

Now Barabbas and the two criminals who were with him in the rebellion and murders were slated to be hanged in the morning hours of Friday, which later became 'Good Friday'.

All these three prisoners, condemned to death were informed about their hanging at least four days earlier, so that they may get ready for the event.

Now out of these prisoners, I believe Barabbas started repenting for his wrong deeds that includes his murders which he committed.

When Barabbas was officially informed about his hanging within few days, I also believe that he must have been in his mid-thirties of his age.

It was Thursday night, which suppose to be the last night for Barabbas because the next day (Friday) morning, he would be hanged on the tree as per standing order of the Roman government

He cried silently and repented, His family came into the picture of his mind and further more he repented, and he said to himself;

"Only if I had not committed murders or led the rebellion against Roman government, I should have been spared with my life."

So these were his thoughts of repentance, while facing the darkness of the night in his prison cell.

I believe that Barabbas also remembered his Creator and confessed to Him for forgiveness of his sins, as he has to face the death on next day morning.

Now let us go to that night in which Lord Jesus Christ was betrayed into the hands of Jews by His own disciple 'Judas', where Jesus was arrested for false accusation of Blasphemy.

It happened to be also the Thursday night when they arrested Jesus Christ, the same night in which the notorious prisoner Barabbas with repenting heart, also waiting sleeplessly, to face the death.

After arresting Jesus Christ, Jews brought Him to the Roman governor 'Pontius Pilate' who was at his palace with a false case of blasphemy.

Now let me take you to the scene of the particular night; It was after midnight and about four hours left to go for the sun rise.

Then all Jews accused Jesus and said, "He has equalled Himself with God by telling that 'He is the Son of God' and then He also said that He could raise the Temple of God within three days of its destruction.

In fact both accusations were false, as He is truly the Son of God by His birth and then He compared His body to the Temple of God, knowing that they will crucify Him to death and He will rise to life on the Third day.

Now 'Pontius Pilate' the governor knew that Jews handed over Jesus Christ to him because of their envy.

There was a custom that the governor used to release one prisoner to the public on the day of the feast of Pass Over which came to fall on the next day (Friday)

The governor 'Pontius Pilate' taking the occasion to release a prisoner, he asked them and said, "Whom do you want me release to you?, Barabbas or Jesus who is called Christ? They shouted, Barabbas!

Then Pilate asked them, "What then shall I do with Jesus, who is called Christ? They all cried and said to him, "Let Him be crucified"

When Pilate saw that, he could not prevail at all but rather that a tumult was raising, he took water and washed his hands before the multitude saying, I am innocent of the blood of this Man. You see to it. (Mathew 27: 24)

Then he released Barabbas to them and when he had scourged Jesus, he delivered Him to be crucified.(Mathew 27:26)

Now the time was about 5 A.M. early morning on Friday, when the governor signed the release document of Barabbas and also the death order to crucify Jesus Christ, the Lord on the Cross.

Jesus Christ, being God knew that who was Barabbas, also knew that he was repenting in his prison cell and few hours away from the death, had a compassion on Barabbas to save him from death.

Now let us go to the prison, where Barabbas almost prepared himself to face the death. And now the time was about 6A.M. and glimpses of the rays of the sun started penetrating the cell where he was.

Barabbas heard the footsteps of the soldiers coming towards his cell and heard someone unlocking the door of his cell.

He thought and said to himself, It is a matter of few hours to suffer on the cross and die and then there won't be pain at all.

Now one of the soldiers having a copy of the release document of the Barabbas shouted and said to him, "Barabbas, you are free man today! Here is the release order for you!"

"Jesus Christ" has taken place of you, and He will be crucified today along with your two accomplices who were with you in the rebellion.

Tears started rolling down from the eyes of Barabbas. He could not believe that such a grace from God, without measure can come on sinner like him.

He praised the Lord God Almighty!, for the 'Deliverance' not only from the death, but also from the eternal condemnation.

So, now you know who the Deliverer Is?

Doubtlessly, it is the Lord Jesus Christ!

He has suffered and died for our sins and paid the price of atonement for us, so that we can be free from the eternal condemnation and death. Praise the Lord!

———————————————————————

9. THE SUFFERINGS OF ISRAEL

When we start to find out the sufferings of Israel, let us go to the period before the Christ Era(B.C.) to the beginning of Israel.

Abraham, the father of Nation Israel, was seventy five years of age, when he left his city 'Haran' and the country Mesopotamia to come to 'Canaan', the present Israel.

The Lord God appeared to Abraham and promised saying that his descendants will be given whole land from the river 'Nile' of Egypt and to the great river Euphrates. (Refer Genesis 15:18)

Well, my brothers and sisters, Abraham lived in the stranger, but could not own the land except a bit of small ground to bury his own dead.

He has wandered from a place to place, with his household, flocks, herds and servants. He has lived in the tents all the days' of his life in the Promised Land and then he died.

Not only that, his son 'Isaac' and his grandson 'Jacob' also lived there as the strangers all over the Promised Land, but could not inherit any land in the Canaan, except the burial ground purchased by Abraham.

Now 'Jacob' along with his twelve sons and their families, migrated to Egypt because of famine and further came to know that 'Joseph', his son was the governor of the Egypt.

Well, everything was alright for the Israelites for about seventy years that was when Joseph was the governor in the land of Egypt.

But when he died, there arose a new king in Egypt, who enslaved all the Israelites and afflicted them ruthlessly.

The new king Pharaoh, set task masters over the Israelites and over burdened them in their daily work to afflict them more and more.

These task masters made Israelites life 'bitter' with bondage and extracted work to make bricks, mortar and all other works of the field.

Further Pharaoh the king of Egypt, instructed two of the Hebrew midwives to kill all the male babies of Israelites, the moment they were born, while they were attending deliveries.

But these Midwives feared God and they did not carry out the order of the king and instead of killing, they saved all male babies of the Israelites.

So Pharaoh, the king of Egypt commanded all his people (Egyptians) to throw away every male child of the Hebrews into the

"Nile River" and leave alone the female babies

In this manner, King Pharaoh and Egyptians treated all Israelites. Their slavery and oppression continued for about four hundred years in Egypt.

When they cried out to the Lord their God Almighty, He has sent Moses to deliver them from their bondage and slavery.

The following scripture of the Bible will clear our doubts if any that who the people of Israel are?

And the Lord said," I have surely seen the oppression of My people Israel, who are in Egypt and have heard their cry, because of their task masters for I know their sorrows" (Exodus 3:7)

These were the words of God, when He spoke to Moses from the burning bush, when He appeared and instructed him to go and deliver His people from the hands of Pharaoh and Egyptians.

So out of four hundred years of their stay in Egypt, Israelites suffered not less than three hundred and thirty years of slavery and oppression.

Now let us come to the forty years of tribulation period in the deserts, where Israelites were led by Moses, the servant of God before they could they could come into the promised land, the present Israel.

When Israelites came out of Egypt, they were about two million people out of which about six hundred thousand people were fighting men, that is between twenty to sixty (20-60) years of age.

They were in the desert 'Shur' and the waters of Marah at this desert were bitter, so they could not drink them.

So they cried out to the Lord and then God has made these bitter waters into sweet waters, trough the hands of Moses His servant.

Now their food and provisions carried by hem were exhausted   completely within a month, and there was nothing to eat.

Just imagine! How it could be possible for Moses to feed two million people in the deserts?

Also imagine the volume of mental stress through which the people of Israel must have suffered at that time.

Then there was a occasion, when out of twelve spies sent to Canaan by Moses to bring him a report, so he can invade the land, only two spies that is Joshua and Caleb gave correct report and encouraged Israelites to invade the land immediately.

Now all the assembly of Israel did not believe, these two men and took the words of other spies, who lied for the sake of fear and advised the Assembly of Israel to turn back to Egypt.

So, all the Israelites rebelled against Moses and their God Almighty Where the Lord sworn by Himself declaring that none of the Israelites, who are twenty years and above except Joshua and Caleb will enter into the Promised Land.

Therefore only children below twenty years of age at that time, after forty years crossed the Jordan River along with Joshua & Caleb entered the Promised Land.

Rest of all Israelites were perished in the deserts and were buried there for their rebellion against Moses according to the oath sworn by the Lord God Almighty.

Then Joshua, who succeeded Moses, took about six years to conquer all the land of Canaan and distribute it to all tribes of Israel according to the word of God.

But one thing he failed to do! That is to destroy all the people of Canaan, when he conquered them. He spared some of them to be servants of Israel and allowed some of beautiful women taken as wives by Israelites which has become snare to them later.

There was a reason why the Lord instructed Moses and Joshua to destroy all the people of Canaan, because of their abominable Idolatries and detestable practices.

Now after the death of Joshua, there was no fear of God among the people of Israel. They were undisciplined and further the women of Canaan, whom they married, led them to the practice of Idol worship of other gods.

The following Scripture of the Bible which came at that time will give us clear picture about Israelites;

"In those days, there was no king in Israel; everyone did what was right in his own eyes" (Judges 17:6)

So, for about three hundred years, during the time of Judges, furthermore, Israelites has suffered, by invasion, plunder and oppression from the surrounding countries.

Now coming to the period of kings who ruled Israel for about four hundred years, Israel lived safely except few curses brought on them by kings like Jeroboam and Ahab who promoted Idolatry among the Israelites.

But there were kings, who ruled Israel justly with fear of God in their hearts.

Here, I want to mention the name of the king David who followed the heart of the Lord and carried out all His commandments.

People of Israel lived very safely in his period of rule and everyone loved king David. He did not allow any pagan customs come into the land of Israel and he ruled the Israel for more than forty years.

Do you know what, God says about the David, when He comes to establish His Heavenly Kingdom on this earth?

Here it is!

"I will establish one shepherd over them and he shall feed them; My servant David, he shall feed them and be their shepherd" (Ezekiel 34:23)

"And I the Lord will be their God and My servant David, a prince among them, I the Lord have spoken." (Ezekiel 34:24)

Then I also want to mention the name of king Josiah, who ruled Judah (Israel) for more than thirty years.

He was the one who became king at the age of eight and by the time he was twelve years old, he ordered and supervised personally the removal of all high places of Idol temples of pagan gods from Jerusalem and other cities of Judah.

What Bible says about him?

"He did what was right in the sight of the Lord and walked in the ways of his father David; He did not turn aside to the right hand to the left" (2 Chronicles 34:2)

Now let us come to the period in which, the kings' rule was ended, and once again Israelites were subjected to exile, slavery and oppression by other nations for about six hundred (600) years, that is from 600 B.C. to the birth of Christ.

It was during the time of 'Jeremiah' the fearless prophet of the Lord who opposed Idolatry throughout his life period.

'Zedekiah' was the king of Judah and he sent his men to Jeremiah the prophet to enquire the Lord, when he was attacked by Nebuchadnezzar, the king of the Babylon.

Then the word of the Lord came, to Zedekiah through Jeremiah the Prophet, saying;

"I will strike the inhabitants of this city (Jerusalem) both man and beast, they shall die of a great pestilence" (Jeremiah 21:6)

"And afterward, says the Lord, "I will deliver Zedekiah king of Judah, his servants and the people, and such as are left in this city from the pestilence and the sword and the famine, into the hand of Nebuchadnezzar king of Babylon, into the hand of their enemies, and into the hand of

those who seek their life and he shall strike them with the edge of the sword. He shall not spare them or have pity or mercy" (Jeremiah 21:7)

"For I have set My face against this city for adversity and not for good, says the Lord; It shall be given into the hand of the king of Babylon, and he shall burn it with fire" (Jeremiah 21:10)

My brothers and sisters!,

Exactly all these things came into the events as the Lord spoken by the mouth of Jeremiah. Then the king Nebuchadnezzar carried away all of their precious gold, silver and also their children in slavery to serve him in his country.

So, in this way Israelites were killed and the rest of them were carried away into captivity to Babylon for the period of seventy (70) years as prophesied by Jeremiah the prophet of God Almighty.

In Babylon, Israelites were subjected to hard labor in the fields of agriculture and construction. Only very few of them were used in the service of the king of Babylon.

They were Daniel, Hananiah, Mishael and Azariah, as they were very young and good looking, having wisdom and knowledge to serve the king in his palace.

They excelled in the service of the king and all other Babylonians (Chaldeans) were envious of these four young Israelites.

At one occasion, when Daniel was away from the Babylon on official work, all his three friends Ananiah, Mishael and Azariah were thrown into the furnace of fire, when these young men refused to worship the Image(Idol) set by the king.

God was faithful to deliver these three young men from the fury of the furnace of fire and from the decree set by the king.

Well on the other occasion, Daniel himself was thrown into the Lion's den by the king's order; because Daniel worshiped the Lord kneeling down towards Jerusalem defying the king's order.

Here also God was faithful to His prophet Daniel to deliver him from the claws and jaws of lions, because he was innocent and blameless in the sight of the Lord.

There was also another occasion where Haman, who was next to the king in the power tried to bring destruction, a catastrophe among the Jews(Israelites) in all one hundred twenty provinces of Babylon kingdom.

But the queen Esther and her uncle Mordecai saved all Jews from the planned catastrophe by Haman with the help of the Lord God Almighty.

So, after seventy years of exile and suffering, Israelites were let go free from Babylon to their city Jerusalem and to their country Israel.

Then under the Persian rule, that is 536 B.C.-332 B.C., the temple at Jerusalem was rebuilt by Zerubabel (descendant of Judah) who returned from Babylon along with Ezra the priest and tens of thousands of Israelites. They rebuilt Jerusalem city and other many cities in Israel and dwelt in them.

Under Greek's Rule 332- 166 B.C.

Then Alexander the great, Emperor of Greece conquered half of the world that includes Israel. When he died suddenly at the age of thirty three (33) yrs, Syria and Israel came under the rule of Selucus who *was one of the generals of Alexander the great.*

During this period, Greek culture was enforced on the Jews that include worshiping of their gods and learning of Greek language.

Further during this period, the Jerusalem Temple was defiled by Antioch king of Syria who ruled Israel from the Damascus.

Under Roman's Rule 63 B.C-313 C.E.

The independence of Jews ended in 63 B.C., when general Pompy of Rome conquered both Syria and Israel.

When Pompy was humiliated by Aristobulus, the king of Israel, he took the Jerusalem city and destroyed it showing his wrath reduced the size of Israel.

During this period only, when Herod was the king of Judea, "Jesus Christ", the

'Messiah' was born in Israel at 'Bethlehem' as per the Scriptures of the Bible. (Refer Micah 5:2)

It was a pity that Israel could not recognise their own 'Messiah' Jesus Christ the Lord, who has ministered to them for three and half (3 ½) years.

They crucified Him on the Cross, because of their ignorance and further it was 'Will of God' to bring the salvation, through Jesus Christ to the whole world.

Now coming back to the history of Israel, all people revolted against Romans in 66-70 C.E. And Jerusalem city was besieged for about four years.

At the end of the siege, the Roman general Titus has broken the walls of Jerusalem, where he killed every one of them by sword and blood flowed out of Jerusalem in streams.

Under Byzantine Rule 313- 636 C.E.

In this period under Emperor Constantine, who adapted Christianity did not allow the Jews to enter Jerusalem, except on one particular day of the year, to mourn the destruction of their Holy Temple.

Under Arab's Rule 637- 1099 C.E.

The Jerusalem and Judea was captured by an Arab general Caliph Omar in 637 C.E. and he brought many Arabs from other countries and settled them in Jerusalem.

Then the Israelites were imposed with heavy taxes by the Arab rulers, thereby most of the Israelites left the country, because they became very poor and could not sustain themselves.

Under Crusader's Rule 1099-1921 C.E.

At the beginning of this period Crusaders from Europe as an army came under the orders of Popes at Rome, recaptured the Jerusalem the holy city from the Arabs (Infidels)

Then they killed many non Christians and Jews, and many were burnt to death and some of them were also sold in slavery.

Under Mamluk(Syrians)Rule1291-1516 C.E.

During this period of Syrians rule, Israel cities were ruined Jerusalem city was abandoned and the remnant of Israel was poverty stricken. This period of rule was darkened by economical instability and plagues and Earthquakes.

Under Ottoman(Turks)Rule 1517- 1917 C.E.

Turks invaded the land of Israel and drove out Mamluk (Syrians).Turks ruled the land of Israel and they divided it into four districts and attached them to the province of Damascus. And from Istanbul, they ruled all provinces including the Israel.

Under The British Rule 1917- 1947 C.E.

In 1917 C.E. British forces ended 'Ottoman's rule in Israel. During this period they allowed Jews from various countries, that is from Russia, Poland, Germany, France, England and Middle East, to come back to their homeland Israel.

During these period II World War took place and most importantly the "Holocaust" meaning "Extermination of Jews" by the Nazi regime headed by 'Hitler' who killed about seven million Jews in the Europe itself.

A Muslim fanatic named 'Haj Amin Al-Hussain' was the Grand Mufti of Jerusalem from 1920-1939 also joined the Hitler in Germany instigating him to kill Jews all over world during these war.

When he has seen that Nazis could not enter Israel, he has called all Muslims and Arabs through Radio from Germany to go and kill all Jews at Jerusalem and Judea. He also said, "Allah is pleased to see Jews spilling their blood and dying."

Thank God, the Lord was with Israel. The United Kingdom and the Unite States of America have also helped Jews to form the State of Israel in 1948, which was recognised by United Nations immediately.

-

10. THE DELIVERANCE OF ISRAEL

On the subject, The Deliverance of Israel, here I want to bring an event in which the Lord has used 'Gideon', the Abizerite from Oprah in Israel.

It was during the time of Judges ruling Israel, after they came out from Egypt and taken over the land of Canaan, Midianites, Amalekites, and Eastern people (Arabs) raided Israel and plundered at their will.

Not only that, they destroyed the standing crops and raided threshing floors and carried away produce of their land. So, Israelites prepared shelters, in mountain caves and strong holds to escape their attacks.

In this situation one day Gideon was threshing wheat in his wine press to keep it away from the Midianites and at that moment;

The angel of the Lord appeared to Gideon and said, "The Lord is with you, mighty warrior!" (Judges 6:12)

But Sir, Gideon replied, "If the Lord with us, why has all this happened to us? Where are all His wonders that fathers told us about? When they said, did not the Lord bring us out of the Egypt? But now the Lord has abandoned us and put us in the hands of Midianites! (Judges 6:13)

The Lord turned to him and said, "Go in the strength you have and save Israel, out of the Midianites hand; "AM I not with you!" (Judges 6:14)

But Lord, Gideon asked, "How can I save Israel? My clan is the weakest in Manasseh! And I am the least in my family"(Judges6:15)

The Lord answered, "I will be with you and you will strike down all the Midianites together"(Judges 6:16)

Now believing the word of the Lord, Gideon blew Trumpet and mustered about thirty thousand men from Asher, Zebulun and Naphtali besides from his clan Manasseh in Israel.

After gathering them together, Gideon and his men rose early in the morning and camped at the spring of Harod. The camp of Midianites and their allied forces were at north to them in the valley below near the hill of Moreh.

Now the Lord said to Gideon, you have too many men for Me to deliver Midianites into your hands. And they should not boost and say, "My own hand has delivered me!"

So ask your own men, who fear of this war and those who fear can go to their houses.

So twenty thousand men left while ten thousand remained.

But the Lord said to Gideon, the people are still many, bring them down to water and I will test them for you there. So he brought them down to the waters.

Now the Lord said to Gideon, that everyone who laps from the water putting their hand to their mouth, you shall set them apart; then those who kneel down to drink the water separately.

And the number of those who lapped putting their hand to the mouth were three hundred, but rest of them got down on their knees to drink water.

Then the Lord said to Gideon, with the three hundred men that lapped, I will save you and give you Midianites in your hand. Let the other men go back to their tents, so they left.

Now the camp of Midianites lay below him in the valley. During that night Lord sent Gideon and his servant Purah to Midianites camp to listen what they were saying about Gideon, so as to encourage him.

When Gideon arrived at the edge of the Midianites camp, a man telling a friend about his dream, I had a dream in that a round loaf of barley bread, came tumbling into the Midianites camp; It struck the tent with such a force that the tent overturned and collapsed.

Then his friend replied that this can be nothing other than the 'Sword of Gideon', son of Joash the Israelite. God has given the Midianites and the whole camp into his hands.

After listening to these conversation, Gideon was encouraged and came back to his amp and said, 'Arise for the Lord has delivered the Midianites into our hands'.

Then he divided them into three companies and put a trumpet into every man's hand with empty pitchers and torches inside the pitchers.

He said to them, when I come to the edge of their camp, you shall do as I do; when I blow the trumpet, then you shall also the blow trumpets on every side of the whole camp and say, "The sword of the Lord and of Gideon."

So after the midnight Gideon and his three hundred men came and surrounded the Midianites at all sides of their camp.

Hearing the trumpet sound from their leader Gideon, the three hundred men blew their trumpets and broke the pitchers. They held the torches in their left hands and blew from their right hand and they cried, "The sword of the Lord and of Gideon."

Then the whole army of Midianites and their allies Amalekites and Arabs cried out for their life and fled in that midnight.

Most importantly when the men of Gideon blew the trumpets, the Lord set every Midianites sword against his companion in their whole camp and many thousands were fallen dead.

Hearing this news, then all Israelites gathered together from Napthali, Asher and Manasseh pursued and killed Midianites and their two kings and two princes.

So, the Lord delivered Israel from their enemies' oppression by the hand of Gideon the Abizerite from Oprah in the Israel.

Now bringing you to another event, how the Lord God Almighty, delivered Israel from the hands of 'Sennacherib' king of

Syria during the period of Isaiah the prophet of God.

It was Hezekiah, the king of Judah ruled Judea at that time from Jerusalem, the city where the Temple of God existed.

The king Hezekiah did what was right in the sight of the Lord according to all that his forefather David has done in Israel.

He removed the high places of Baal and broke sacred pillars of Ashtoreth and cut down the wooden images of all detestable gods worshiped by Israelites.

He made it compulsory that people should come and worship the Lord at the Jerusalem Temple.

Now in the fourteenth year of the king Hezekiah, Sennacherib the king of Assyria came up against all fortified cities of Judah and took them.

Then Sennacherib sent his captain Rabshakah with great army to the king Hezekiah at Jerusalem, where he was able to speak only to the servants of King Hezekiah who were standing on the wall near the Main gate.

There Rabshakah said to them, to say to Hezekiah, the king of Judah, thus says the great king of Assyria! What confidence is this you trust, having plans and power for war?

Look!, You are trusting in the staff of broken reed of Egypt on which if man leans, it will go into his hand and pierce it; So is Pharaoh king of Egypt, to all who trust in him.

But if you say to me, we trust in the Lord our God; Is it not He whose high places and whose alters, Hezekiah has taken away? And said to Judah and Jerusalem, you shall worship only before this alter.

Now therefore, I urge you, give pledge to my master the king of Assyria and I will give you two hundred horses; If you are able on your part to put riders on them!

How then, you will repel one captain of the least of my master's servants and put trust in Egypt for chariots and horse men?

Now when servants of Hezekiah brought all these words of Sennacherib king of Assyria to him, he tore his cloths and went into the temple of God to pray for the deliverance.

Then he has sent two of his servants to prophet Isaiah further to lift up his prayer to the Lord to save the remnant that is left in Jerusalem.

After listening the messages of Hezekiah, Isaiah the prophet sent them back to the king Hezekiah saying, Thus says the Lord, 'Do not be afraid of the words with which you have heard by the servant of the king

Assyria who have blasphemed Me'. (Isaiah 37: 6)

"Whom have you reproached and blasphemed? Against whom have you raised your voice? And lifted up your eyes on high? Against the Holy One of Israel?" (Isa 37:23)

Therefore thus says the Lord, concerning the king of Assyria;

"He shall not come into this city; Nor shot an arrow there!; Nor come before it with shield; Nor build a siege mound against it." (Isaiah 37: 33)

By the way that he came; By the same he shall return; And he shall not come onto this city, says the Lord. For I will defend this city to save it, for My own sake and for My servant David's sake. (Isa 37:34-35)

Then the angel of the Lord went out from Him and killed one hundred eighty five thousand in the camp of the Assyrians. When the rest of the troops got up in the morning, they have seen corps all around their camp lying dead.

So, Sennacherib king of Assyria departed with humility and gone back to his country with rest of his troops and remained at Nineveh.

Now to bring the word of the Lord into deed, one day when Sennacherib, king of Assyria had gone into the temple of Nisroch his god to worship, he was slain by his own sons Adramalech and Sherezar.

Here, I want to call the attention of the nations plotting against Israel! Listen carefully; Is there any authority above God in the universe? Is there any power mightier than God?

Even the Devil, who is called Satan, the contender for power knows about his certain destruction at the end.

If it is so, who will oppose God from saving Zion?

I know for certain that God is with Israelites who are building the cities of Israel in these last days of this earth. I am also sure that the descendants of Jacob will inherit the land of Israel and posses it forever. Amen.

Now let us see what the Lord says by the mouth of Isaiah the prophet of God, about Israel?

But now says the Lord who created you O Jacob!, And He who formed you, O Israel, fear not for I have redeemed you. I have called you by your name and you are Mine. (Isaiah 43:1)

Fear not for I am with you, I will bring your descendants from East and gather you from the West. I will say to the North, "Give them up and to the South, and don't keep them back. Bring My sons from afar and My daughters from the ends of the earth. (Isaiah 43:5&6)

The important aspect of Isaiah's prophecy is that the Lord has brought back the descendants of Israel, from North that is from Russia before and after the 1st and 2nd world wars between 1903 to1947 of the Christ Era.

Then from the West, that is from Europe and America, especially from the Germany before and after the 2nd world war.

And then from East that is from Iran, Iraq, Jordan, Syria and Arabia between 1948 to 1952 of Christ Era, and from South that is from Egypt before Israel's independence.

So, God once again raised the Israel as a nation in 1948 and the entire world know the rest of the history of Israel from 1948 to till now.

Now let us see what the Lord has said by the mouth of Jeremiah the prophet of God, after the period of Isaiah.

"Thus speaks the Lord God of Israel saying; Write in a book for yourself all the words that I have spoken to you. (Jeremiah 30:2)

For behold the days are coming, says the Lord, that I will bring back from captivity My people Israel and Judah, says the Lord. And I will cause them to return to the land that I gave to their fathers, and they shall posses it." (Jeremiah 30:3)

My brothers and sisters, see here the Lord God telling Jeremiah to make a record of His saying that He will bring all His people

Judah and Israel from the nations to which He has driven them earlier.

Further He also declares that Israelites will return to the land of their fathers to whom the Lord God has given it as an inheritance.

Now, coming to the word of the Lord spoken by the prophet Ezekiel about the root cause for the exile of Israelites and God's promise of restoration of Israel at the end, let us go to the Scriptures of Bible.

"Son of man, when the house of Israel dwelt in their own land, they defiled it by their own ways and deeds; To Me their way was like the uncleanness of a woman in her customary impurity."

Therefore I poured out My fury on them for the blood they had shed on the land and for their idols with which they had defiled it.

So I scattered them among the nations, and they were dispersed throughout the countries; I judged them according to their ways and their deeds. (Ezekiel 36:17- 19)

The Lord God has driven them out of their own land, not for any silly reasons; But to uphold His Holy Name for the fear and righteousness among His people and the Gentiles.

See my brothers and sisters, they were worshiping detestable idols and shedding the blood of innocent people of Israel at that time.

But now let us go to the prophecies of reconciliation of the people of Israel with the Lord their God at the end times of this earth.

"For I will take you from among the nations, gather you out of all countries and

bring you back in to your own land. (Ezekiel 36:24)

Then I will sprinkle clean water on you and you shall be clean; I will cleanse you from all your filthiness and from your idols. (Ezek36:25)

I will give you new heart and put you a new spirit within you, I will take the heart of the stone out of your flesh and give you a heart of Flesh.(Ezekiel 36:26)

"Then you shall dwell in the land that I gave to your fathers, you shall be My people and I will be your God." (Ezekiel 36:28)

So my brothers and sisters, I am calling upon you to implore the above promises of the Lord God; Further I am asking you that which of the promises of the Lord in this regard has failed?

Do you not see the Israel as a nation now?;
The wonderful acts of God through His
Spirit motivated and moved Israelites to go
from all the corners of the world, to the
land of their forefathers to rebuild and
posses it.

From 1948 to till date, you know the
history of Israel; It's development not only
in the field of science and technology but
also in the agriculture, so as to make it self
sufficient in food security for its citizens.

Now coming to the New Testament of
Bible, let us go to the Scriptures of God
which came through St.Paul, one of the
Apostles of Lord Jesus Christ, concerning
the salvation of people of Israel.

I say then, have they (Israelites) stumbled
that they should fail? Certainly not!, But
through their fall, to provoke them to
jealousy, Salvation has come to the
Gentiles.(Romans 11:11)

Now if their fall is riches for the world and their failure riches for the Gentiles how much more their fullness. (Romans 11:12)

For I speak to you Gentiles, in as much as I am an Apostle to the Gentiles, I magnify my ministry. (Romans 11: 13)

If by any means I may provoke to jealousy those (Israelites) who are my flesh and save some of them. (Romans 11:14)

For I do not desire, brethren (Gentile) that you should be ignorant of this mystery, lest you should be wise in your own opinion, that blindness 'in part' has happened to Israel until the fullness of the Gentiles has come.(Romans 11:25)

And so, "All Israel will be saved" as it is written "The Deliverer will come out of Zion" And He will turn away ungodliness from Jacob. (Romans 11:26)

So my dear gentile brothers and sisters, let us thank God first for His Salvation and then also thank our Israeli brothers and sisters, by whose ignorance and rejection of their "Messiah" Salvation has come to us!.

It does not mean God has rejected Israel totally, His beloved people! But provoking them to jealousy, when they see even Gentiles are being saved by His grace.

Who has suffered for the sake of 'Salvation of God'? Is it Gentiles of this world? Not at all!

Is it not His chosen people, Abraham, Isaac, Jacob and their descendants?

Is it not the twelve Apostles (Israelites) chosen by the Lord Jesus Christ? Whom He has sent throughout the world to preach the Gospel of the goodness of coming Heavenly Kingdom!

Then who were killed in Millions, that is during the 'Holocaust' under Dictator Hitler in the 2nd world war?

Is it not the Jews? Yes it is!

Then whose country or say which city in the world was attacked for more than forty (40) times in the human history?

Is it not Israel and the city Jerusalem? Yes it is!

So, my Israeli and Jewish brethren, you are not a curse! But a blessing to the whole world!, because it is written;

"Through Abraham, all the families and the nations of this earth shall be blessed" (Refer Genesis 18:18)

11. THE SECOND ELIJAH

"And if you are willing to accept it, he is Elijah who was to come"(Mathew 1:14)

Well! These were the words of the Lord Jesus Christ, when He said about "John the Baptist" who was baptising the people in Jordan river and preaching 'Repentance' just before Jesus was revealed to John.

Now there was "One Elijah" during the times of the kings period in Israel history, precisely when the king Ahab was ruling the Israel.

This Elijah was deadly against the Idol worship of pagan gods by Israelites during his life period.

The first Elijah in his "One Day Act" that is after performing a miracle at the 'Mount Carmel' not only executed eight hundred fifty (850) prophets and priests of false gods, but also turned the hearts of all Israelites towards their Lord, the true God.

There is a prophecy from "Malachi" the last prophet of the Old Testament of the Bible, telling that Elijah will be sent by God again to turn the hearts of the people before the Dreadful Day of the Lord, comes on the earth.

But the "Dreadful Day Of The Lord" has not yet come on this earth; So, the "John Baptist" who was described by the Lord Jesus Christ is in fact the "Second Elijah."

Now let us go to the Scriptures of the Bible, whether there is provision for the "Second Elijah."

After the transfiguration of Jesus Christ, His Apostles Peter, James and John who has witnessed the event and also seen Elijah and Moses talking to the Lord Jesus Christ, had a question in their mind.

Now let us see, what they asked Lord Jesus Christ?

"And they asked Him saying, why do the Scribes say that Elijah must come first". (Mark 9:11)

Then He answered and told them, "Indeed Elijah is coming first and restore all things". (Mark 9:12)

But I say to you that Elijah has also come, and they did to him, whatever they wished as it is written of him. (Mark 9:13)

So, according to these Scriptures, Indeed the Elijah will come well in time before the "Dreadful Day of the Lord" comes on the earth, to turn the hearts of the people towards the Lord God Almighty.

Further, these Scriptures also says that Elijah had come already, and they did to him, what? That is beheaded him as they wished!.

Now you know, about whom I am speaking? Yes! Doubtlessly about John the Baptist only!

Now there are other Scriptures also, faithfully telling us that John Baptist is in fact the Second Elijah and let us go straight to the Scriptures.

But the Angel (Gabriel) said to him," Do not be afraid Zacharias, for your prayer is heard and your wife Elizabeth will bear you a son and you shall call his name John. (Luke 1:13)

For, he will be great in the sight of the Lord, and shall drink neither wine, nor strong drink. He will also be filled with the Holy Spirit, even from his mother's womb.(Luke 1:15)

And he will turn many of the children of Israel to the Lord their God (Luke 1:16)

He will also go before Him, "In the spirit and power of Elijah" to turn the hearts of the fathers to the children and disobedient to the wisdom of the just, to make ready a people prepared for the Lord (Luke 1:17)

Praise the Lord!, Now I hope that I have led you correctly to the point!, Am I right?

Yes!

The angel Gabriel cannot lie, because when he was speaking to the Zacharias, father of John Baptist, he was speaking in the presence of God.

And further Lord Jesus Christ has confirmed that John Baptist is in fact the Second Elijah, because "John Baptist was in the Spirit and Power of Elijah".

Now what was foretold about John Baptist in the Old Testament of the Bible?

For that we will have to go back to the book of Isaiah fortieth (40th) chapter; Let us see what was written of him?

The voice of one crying in the wilderness; "Prepare the way of the Lord; Make straight in the desert, a high way for our God" (Isaiah40:3)

Here, God has granted to see the days of "John Baptist" by Isaiah, when he prophesied about him.

Now coming to the point, who has cried in the wilderness? Telling the people, "Repent for the kingdom of heaven is at hand!", Of course it is none other than the John Baptist.   Praise the Lord!

Moreover, all the four authors of New Testament of the Bible, inspired by the Holy Spirit, speaks the same thing about John Baptist, is the one about whom Isaiah prophesied many centuries before.

Not only that, Jesus Christ Himself stands as witness telling people that "John Baptist" is the one who has been sent just before Him, to prepare the way for Him.

Now let us see, why John Baptist is called the Second Elijah?

The first Elijah, vehemently opposed "Ahab" the king of Israel and the queen "Jezebel" his wife regarding Idol worship and Adultery.

And then the first Elijah turned the hearts of people of Israel from worshiping pagan gods Chemosh and Baal, to the Lord, the true God when he has performed the Miracle on the Mount Carmel.

Now, John Baptist also turned the hearts of people of Israel, by preaching 'Repentance' and baptising them in the waters of Jordan River, when many of Israelites were worshiping Roman and Greek gods and corrupted by the pagan customs.

Lastly, the very important and truthful point is that soon after Elijah turned the hearts of the people of Israel from Idolatry, the Lord God revealed Himself to Elijah at the Mount Horeb.

Now in the same manner, at the end of John Baptist's ministry, God revealed Himself at the Jordan River, where John Baptist has seen the glory of God in Jesus Christ, who was in the flesh.

Going back to the Scriptures from the book of Malachi, chapter 4 and verse 6 of the Bible which says, "And he(Elijah) will turn the hearts of the fathers to the children, and the hearts of the fathers to the children".

Now coming to the word of God about John Baptist, "He will also go before the

Lord, In the spirit and power of Elijah to turn the hearts of the fathers to the children. (Luke 1:17)

Please carefully note here that John Baptist has done exactly first half part of the job of Elijah suppose to do, that is turning the hearts of the fathers to the children.

And leaving other part of the job, that is turning the hearts of the children to their fathers to the Last Elijah who will appear in time before the Dreadful Day of the Lord comes on the earth.

_____-

12. AN EXAMPLES FOR GOD'S GRACE

Now, let me take you to a couple of events recorded in the Bible, That is how the grace of God came on sinners just in time, before their imminent destruction and death, so they escaped wrath of God and condemnation into the Hell.

Let us go to the first event:-

It was during the time of the kings in Israel. Jeroboam, son of Joash was the king over Israel and he reigned forty one years at Samaria.

During his rule, he has recaptured Damascus to Hamath, cities which were belonged Judah earlier. So, 'Nineveh' also was one of the great city came under the rule of the king of Israel.

Now majority of the people of Nineveh were Gentiles, who did not know the Lord, the true God. But they heard about Him through Israelites, about His wonderful deeds and miracles by which He led them from Egypt to Canaan.

At this juncture, the Lord God has called prophet Jonah, son of Amittai saying, "Arise go to Nineveh the great city and cry out against it, for their wickedness has come up before Me." (Jonah 1:2)

But instead of going to Nineveh, Prophet Jonah fled to "Tarsish" by a ship because he thought Nineveh people will not listen to him and further he feared that they may kill him as they are Gentiles.

Now the prophet Jonah was sailing in a ship to Tarsish against the will of God. So the Lord was displeased with him and sent out a great storm to de-stabilise the ship and the ship was about to break.

When all the sailors and inmates were running here and there on the board of the ship out of fear, Jonah was sleeping in the lower deck as he does not know anything about the storm.

When the captain of the ship saw Jonah sleeping, he became angry and woke him up and said, "Call upon your God, perhaps He may consider us and save us from this storm."

And they said to one another, "Come let us cast lots that we may know for whose cause this trouble has come upon us". So they cast lots and the lot fell on Jonah.(Jonah 1:7)

Then Jonah said to the captain and others, "Pick me up and throw me into the sea; Then the sea will become calm for you, for I know that this great tempest is because of me. (Jonah 1:12)

So, they picked up Jonah and threw him into the sea and sea ceased from its raging. (Jonah 1:15)

Then the men feared the Lord exceedingly and offered a sacrifice to the Lord and took vows. (Jonah 1: 16)

Now, the Lord commanded the great fish (whale) to swallow Jonah. And Jonah was in the belly of the fish for three days and three nights.

Then Jonah prayed to the Lord God, from the belly of the fish saying "Forgive me O' Lord God; I have sinned against You and I will never again disobey You."

"Have a mercy on me and release me from the pangs of the death. Then I will go back to Nineveh and do your will as per Your word".

So the Lord spoke to the fish and it vomited Jonah into a dry ground (Jonah2:10)

Now my brothers and sisters, we have come to the half part of the event, But yet not to the main event!

What I want to tell you, from the half part of this event is, the Lord God Almighty disciplined His prophet Jonah, who was rebellious, into obedience to do His will.

Then taking the opportunity of Jonah's disobedience, the Lord God brought fear among the sailors and travellers of the ship bound to Tarsish.

And then by bringing a calmness to the raging sea, "Acceptance of the Lord as true God by them, when they sacrificed to Him and took vows on His name. Praise the Lord!

Now let us come to the main event of the action by Jonah that is, how he carried out the will of God and what was the outcome of it?

So, Jonah arose and came to Nineveh, the great city to preach the message of the Lord.

And Jonah began to enter the city on the day's walk. Then he cried out and said, "Yet forty days and Nineveh shall be overthrown" (Jonah 3:4)

Prophet Jonah preached to the people of Nineveh, not only the message of God, but also his bitter experience when he fled from the presence of the Lord, that is for not carrying out His will.

He narrated to them, about the events that took place on the ship while he fled to Tarsish and also about his deliverance from the death by the Lord, when he prayed from the belly of the great fish (whale).

Now the city was very big and it took three days for Jonah to go all over the city

Nineveh and preach the message of God; that is about its imminent destruction.

Then Jonah went out from the East side of the city and sat down on a rock facing the city, to see what would become of it within those forty days.

When the king of Nineveh heard the word of God, he covered himself with sack cloths and sat down on ashes and repented for his sins and wickedness.

He also ordered the people to repent for their sins and wickedness and fallow him wearing sack cloths and sitting on the ashes to pray for their deliverance.

So, everyone in the city of Nineveh feared the Lord God and repented truly and conducted themselves as decreed by their king.

Then God saw their work that they turned from their evil ways and God relented from

the disaster that He had said, He would bring upon them and did not do it.
(Jonah 3:10)

So, my brothers and sisters, see what has happened to the people of Nineveh? Did they not escape the wrath of God?

Yes! By the grace of God Almighty!

When the Lord God has seen the true repentance of the people of Nineveh, that is after Prophet Jonah preached the message of destruction, God has relented from bringing destruction to the people.

Now let us come to the second event which took place in the New Testament of Bible, where grace of God came on a sinner who was about to die an hour on the cross.

I think, most of the Christians know about whom, I am going to mention here;

Yes!, You are right!, It is about the robber (criminal) who was crucified along with the Lord Jesus Christ on the Good Friday.

Before going to this event, I want to quote a Scripture from the Bible about the "Grace of God" and here it is;

"I will be gracious to whom I will be gracious and I will have compassion on whom I will have compassion" (Exodus 33:19)

My brothers and sisters, what do you understand from the above Scripture of the Bible?

Here it is! "Showing a grace is prerogative of the Lord God Almighty" No one can question Him, why He is showing grace to someone while not showing on the other?

But there is a common platform set by God to everyone to receive His grace; that is true repentance for our sins and acceptance of Jesus Christ as our Lord and Savior through our faith.

We cannot cheat God Almighty, by our hypocrisy and false humiliations to receive His grace. The Lord God Almighty is wise and knows everyone by their hearts and thoughts that what are concealed in them.

Now coming to the event, we do not know names of the two criminals who were crucified along with the Lord Jesus Christ.

But we do know the name of their leader that is Barabbas who escaped death on the same Good Friday, because of the Lord's Grace.

These two criminals were part of the Barabbas gang, who were rebellious against the Roman government at that time in Israel.

They must have heard about Jesus Christ and about His Apostles, because the Lord preached the Gospel for more than three years not only in Israel but also in the surrounding nations.

Then they must have also heard about His Miracles which He performed among the people, even about the "Lazar" who was raised to life from his tomb after four days of his death.

If they known all these things about Jesus Christ, then they must have also known that He was righteous, preached non-violence and not involved in any crime.

Now let us go to the Scene, where Jesus Christ was hanging on the Cross and the two criminals also crucified one on left and the other on right side of the Lord.

Then one of the criminals who was hanging along with the Lord, has blasphemed the Lord saying, "If You are Christ, save Yourself and us" (Luke 23:39)

But the other criminal, rebuked him saying, "Do you not even fear God, seeing you are under the same condemnation?" (Luke 23:40)

"And we indeed justly, for we receive the reward of our deeds, but this Man has done nothing wrong" (Luke 23:41)

Then he said to Jesus, "Lord, remember me when You come into Your Kingdom"(Luke 23:42)

And Jesus said to him, "Assuredly I say to you, today you will be with Me in Paradise" (Luke 23:43)

My brothers and sisters, see how one of the criminal, blasphemed the Lord, though he was in pain, like the other, yet he mocked the Lord Jesus saying, "If You are the Christ, save Yourself and us"

And also note how the other criminal, rebuked his friend immediately, saying that they rightly deserve the death punishment, but not Jesus Christ! Because He is righteous.

So, the other criminal who has rebuked his friend, has repented for all his sins, just before his death on the cross has been delivered from the condemnation of the Hell and assured a place in the Paradise.

It means the repented criminal was revealed by the Holy Spirit about Jesus Christ's divine nature and he believed in Him whole heartedly just before his death.

Seeing his repentant heart, for all his sins with confession and acceptance of Himself as Savior, Lord Jesus Christ said to him, "Assuredly I say to you, today you will be with Me in Paradise".

What a wonderful promise! That is by a Creator Himself to a sinner who just repented one hour before his death.

I imagine myself being in the place of that criminal who repented with his heart and believed in the Lord Jesus Christ!

So, my brothers and sisters! Repent for your sins and wickedness today itself as we do not know the day of our death.

And the promise of the Lord is not only for that repentant criminal, but also to every one of us, who should be like him for the faith in the Lord.

—

13. SELF WITNESS TO THE GOD'S GRACE

Now coming to explain the "Grace of God" in my life, there were four incidents rather accidents from which I was saved by the Lord Jesus Christ by "His Grace".

First Accident:-

I was about six (6) years old at that time and on one summer day; I went from my village, along with my relatives aged between 10 to 12 years to a nearby open well to witness their swimming talents.

All of them were amateurish swimmers, but not myself and I was eager to learn swimming in that tender age which is in fact the ideal age where one should learn swimming.

There was a aunt named Rosalie who was about 10 years old, also swimming in that well. I was sitting by the edge of the waters of the well and watching delightfully.

Then I was overwhelmed by the eagerness to learn swimming, I have slipped into the waters of the well, unnoticed by anyone.

There I was drowning in that well and I was desperately trying to come up. The fear creeped into my little mind about the danger of the death.

At that moment, I was caught behind by my collar of the shirt and pulled out of the waters safely. Later I came to know that it was my Aunt Rosalie acted as an angel of God and saved my life.

Now, what do you think my brothers and sisters?, Is it not "Grace of God" saved me, when I acted foolishly not knowing the danger of drowning and death?

Yes!

Without any doubt only by "Grace of God"! He who created me does not want me to die at that tender age of my life.

"Thank you Lord Jesus Christ, O' my God! And I will never forget this incident as I want to be a witness to the people of this world for Your amazing grace

Second Accident:-

And coming to the second incident in my life, where I faced drowning like situation in the "Beas River" which is in Himachal Pradesh (India) in 1986.

Well!, I was serving in the Indian Air Force at that time and we, total six IAF personnel, undertook the 'First Kayaking Expedition of India" in the "Beas River" and I was a good swimmer.

We were accompanied by support staff that included drivers, cooks and telecommunication staff with vehicles and wireless sets.

Besides this, there were also two instructors and two rescuers from the Western Himalayan Mountaineering Institute (WMHI) to help us to complete the Expedition successfully.

The River Beas at Manali in Himachal Pradesh is very dangerous, as it has got lot of rocks and steep waterfalls flowing downwards towards the Kullu valley.

I think, it was on the second day of our expedition, where I was kayaking through Rapids (fast flowing white waters) sitting in my kayak (fibre glass boat) and manoeuvring it with hand pedals.

Now suddenly, I came across a rock and my kayak got capsized in that fast flowing white waters and I was under waters upside down for a moment.

Then, I wriggled out myself free from the kayak and I was carried away in the Rapids of the River which flowed at the speed not less than forty kmph. I could feel my legs hitting boulders underneath the waters.

I noticed that both rescuers running along the river bank to throw life rings to me. And then I was coming down near the dangerous patch of Rapids which was about hundred meters away from me.

When the first life guard (rescuer) thrown his life ring to me, I just missed it. And further, I was dragged towards that dangerous patch of Rapids by the gravity of the waters flow.

Now the second life guard threw his life ring to me, just in front of me and in right time, so I caught hold of it and cried out saying, "Thank You Jesus, my Lord!"

Then I was pulled away safely, to the bank of the river, just in time, so I did not go through that dangerous patch (Rapids) of the river.

What my point here is that, If I had gone through those dangerous patch of Rapids, I might have been killed and if not then severely wounded myself with multiple fractures in my body.

Now I feel that, the life ring thrown to me, was the "Sceptre of Grace" of our Lord Jesus Christ, by which I was saved from those turbulent rapids of the Beas River.

So, these were two drowning accidents which took place in my life. The first one was in the still waters near to my village when I was six years old boy and not knew the swimming.

The second one was in the fast flowing waters (Rapids) of Beas River near Manali

(Himachal Pradesh) in 1986 when I was thirty one years old and knowing the swimming very well.

Third Accident:-

Now after two drowning accidents, I have come across two prominent motor accidents in my life, where I might have been killed, but by the grace of God Almighty, I am alive even today.

I think it was in 1993, after my discharge from the Indian Air Force, I was in the transport Business. I had a brand new Oil Tanker Lorry at that time. Sometimes I used to go as a second driver, to ease the burden of the main driver.

Coming to this accident that is after loading our tanker lorry with oil from a trading company that was in Bombay and the goods (oil) to be delivered somewhere near Chennai city. Myself and our main driver and cleaner, altogether we were three in the cabin.

I was driving the vehicle and our main driver was sleeping on the berth behind me and we were nearing Satara (big town) which is adjacent to the National Highway.

It was in the afternoon and the high way was not broad enough unlike these days; but was sufficient for both heavy vehicles to cross safely from the opposite direction.

Now, there was a trailer parked dangerously to the left side of the road from the opposite direction. And I was still away from it and was likely to cross it in 15- 20 seconds.

And at that moment, I noticed a heavy laden truck, coming from the opposite direction and it was also likely to cross the parked trailer at the same time.

I switched on head lights and increased the speed of my vehicle, by pressing on the accelerator pedal, thinking that I will cross the parked trailer first.

But to my horror, I have seen at the same time, the driver of the truck coming from the opposite direction, also switched on his truck's headlights and further proceeded to cross the parked trailer.

It seems, the driver on the opposite side, realised that it was too late to avoid head on collusion and he steered his truck to his left hardly ten meters away from the parked trailer.

Then there was loud noise, and God only knows! How my vehicle came to a halt on the right side of the road without overturning (capsizing). By that time my main driver got up from his sleep in great fear.

Then I saw my right side cabin glass shattered to pieces like crystals and the right side of the cabin smashed. I could also see the steering and control panels damaged to an extent, where one would ask "Is the driver alive?

To my disbelief I was still sitting on the driver seat, holding the steering tightly and my right foot pressing hard on the brake pedal.

Not only that to my amazement, there was not even a single scratch on my body and none of the other two crew members in the cabin suffered any injuries.

Now I remember and recall what I cried when my vehicle crashed on to the truck, coming from the opposite side. The only word that came out from my mouth at that moment was "Jesus!"

Here, I want to quote, couple of Scriptures of the Bible for your reference.

"This poor man cried out and the Lord heard him; And saved him out of all his troubles! (Psalms 34:6)

The angel of the Lord encamps all around those who fears Him and delivers them. (Psalms 34:7)

Further, we should know the meaning for the name Jesus, Well it is the title name derived from Hebrew language (Joshua) meaning, 'Lord saves' So, when I cried to the Lord Jesus, He has saved me by His grace from this accident, proving Himself true to His name.

Fourth Accident:-

Now coming to explain my 4th accident that took place in my life in the month of October 2005 near the Chennai Airport.

Well, I was working for Larson & Toubro, at Chennai on contract job as a Chief Security Officer at that period of time, and I used to go to the office daily by motor cycle from Tambaram where I was staying with my family

On that particular day in the evening it was raining and I was returning home from my duty and the time was about 6 .15 P.M.

Now I was near Chennai Airport, riding my motor cycle wearing helmet and rain coat and the speed of my bike was about 40 kmph.

Though I was wearing rain coat and helmet, my hands and legs were wet and the rain was slashing on my face as there was no windshield fixed in my helmet.

As it was a evening time coupled with downpour of the rain, there was a poor visibility all over the place and more over the road also was slippery

After crossing the signal, which shown green light, I might have passed about 30 meters, then my motor bike was hit behind by a speeding car very badly.

Then I was thrown out from my two wheeler and in fact I was flying in the air for a distance of 5 to 6meters and was about to crash land on the road with my head and shoulders down.

Now, before I crash landed on the road, my mouth opened very wide in fear and three words of prayer came out from me instantly; and they are "Jesus save me!"

Then I crash landed on my left shoulder and left side of my face on the road making a big noise. I could see my motor cycle fallen at the centre of the road far behind me.

To my amazement, I heard all drivers behind me applying brakes in their vehicles and further to my relief, I have seen a auto rickshaw driver, coming out of his vehicle to help me!.

After crashing to the ground, I rolled over at least two times and then slowly got up into my feet and looking towards heaven, I cried out saying, Praise the Lord! Praise the Lord! Allelujah!

Now my head was intact inside the helmet and I could not lift my left arm as there was severe pain in my left shoulder and I could see minor abrasions on my left fore arm and left knee.

It was a miraculous save! Allelujah!

You may ask me, how it is a miraculous save?

Here it is! The auto rickshaw driver who was close to me behind, stopped his vehicle strait away and came out and stopped all *other vehicles coming behind, by signalling with his both hands.*

So, I escaped from a run over by a heavy vehicle, came behind and my bike was visible to every driver as it was lying in the centre of the road.

Later on, the same auto rickshaw driver took me to a Orthopaedic Clinic near to my house at Tambaram. After a couple of X-rays taken, the Doctor told me that nothing to worry for except a small crack fracture at my left clavicle bone, which can be healed in 4 to 6 weeks.

So after 6 weeks period including my physiotherapy treatment once again I was fully fit and able to ride the same motor cycle as usual.

Here I want to quote a Scripture of the Bible which says; He said to me, "My grace is sufficient for you, for My strength is made perfect in weakness". Therefore most gladly, I will rather boost in my infirmities that Power of Christ may rest upon me. (2 Corinthians 12:9)

These are the words of the Lord Jesus Christ to His apostle St.Paul when he suffered physical affliction not once but many times in his life for the sake of the Lord Jesus Christ.

But myself a least servant of the Lord Jesus Christ, yet to carry out major part of the will of God, which is pending, also confess all of my weakness to Him, so that He may strengthen me. Amen.

So my brothers and sisters in Christ Jesus our Lord, please do not think, it is because of our self righteousness, we escape some of the grave accidents we face in our life, But only by grace of the Lord God Almighty.

---

14. GRACE FOR THE LAST GENERATION

"For by grace you have been saved through faith and that not of yourself. It is the gift of God."(Ephesians 2:8)

"Not of works lest anyone should boost" (Ephesians 2:9)

My dear brothers and sisters, what do you understand by these two Scriptures of the Bible?

Why should we be saved, "Only by His grace" and not by our works?

What is the primary requirement that God expects from the human beings to save them?

And further what for we should be saved?

Now firstly let us go to the answer for the question, why we should be saved "Only by His grace"

Well, the first man Adam our first humanly father was created by God has fallen into the sin by his disobedience to the Commandment of God.

Adam & Eve were created by God about six thousand (6000) years ago. Adam was created first and then Eve was formed out of a rib taken from the body of Adam when he was in deep sleep.

Let us go to the Scripture of the Bible, which says;

"So, God created man in His own image, In the image of God, He created him; Male and female, He created them" (Genesis 1:27)

After Adam and Eve were created by God, they were put into the gardens of Eden by Him, to live in there peacefully and righteously. The first couple were given authority and dominion over all the earth that is over the beast of the earth birds of the air, and fish of the seas.

To test their faithfulness, God gave the first couple Adam and Eve, only one commandment; that is not to eat the fruit from the tree of knowledge of good and evil, which was also in the Garden of Eden.

So, Adam & Eve, the first couple kept themselves away from this tree and its fruit while they lived in the garden.

Now the "Lucifer" the chief angel, who led the rebellion along with thirty three (33) crores of angels against the Holy God Almighty in the heaven, were cursed and were thrown out from there by God.

This "Lucifer" who is also called Satan and Devil came to the earth along with fallen angels (Demons) and saw Adam & Eve were living righteously with all the blessings of God.

So, Satan became jealous and vowed in his heart to bring destruction and death to the man who was in the image of God.

He came in the form of Serpent with a plan of deception, into the Eden garden to "Eve" when she was alone.

There the Devil who was in the Serpent body asked Eve, "Why do you not eat the fruit from this tree and who told you not to eat this fruit'?

She replied and said, the God who put us in this garden, commanded us not to eat the fruit from this tree and warned us saying, that if we eat, we will surely die.

Now, let us refer the Bible for this fact;

"But of the tree of the knowledge of good and evil, you shall not eat; for in the day that you eat of it; you shall surely die" (Genesis 2:17)

Then Serpent (Devil) said to the Eve, "You will surely not die" (Genesis 3:4)

"For God knows that in the day you eat of it, your eyes will be opened and you will be like God, knowing good and evil" (Genesis 3:5)

The Devil in the body of the Serpent has induced the Eve, by telling her lie that they will not die and will be like God, after eating the forbidden fruit

So, Eve the woman took the fruit from that forbidden tree and ate it and then she gave the fruit of the same tree to her husband Adam who ate it.

By these act, the first couple Adam & Eve rebelled against God, giving an opportunity to the sin to enter the world which has caused the death to the human beings ultimately.

So, the first couple Adam & Eve lost their righteousness to stand before God as they had fallen in the sin by their rebellious act against God.

Further they also forfeited their right and dominion over the earth to the Lucifer that is Satan who deceived them.

Then Cain the elder son of Eve, out of his envy, killed his younger brother Abel who was righteous.

In this way, man defiled himself by his murders, adulteries, robberies and covetousness; and then by his lies and abominable Idol worships.

So, we the descendants of Adam & Eve inherited their sin by birth and then by own sinful deeds, have fallen victims of the death.

Let us see what the Bible says regarding this;

Therefore, first as through one man 'sin' entered the world and death through 'sin' and this death spread to all men because all sinned.(Romans 5:12)

There was no one on the earth who was righteous to save the sinful man from the curse of the death.

But only God could save the man, as He only is Righteous and Holy!; And even angels of the heaven could not do anything in this matter.

So, the Lord God willed Himself to come in the name of Jesus Christ to redeem us from our sins, then from the curse of death ultimately.

God loved the man because, he is in His own image; Let us see what the Bible tells us in this regard?

"For God so loved the world, that He gave His only begotten Son, that whoever

believes in Him should not perish, but have everlasting life" (John 3:16)

And now, Can anyone be saved from the judgement of God?

No one at all!

If God judges the man, not even Abraham, "The Father of the Faith" could enter into the kingdom of God with eternal life.

So, the Lord God provided a way for the sinful man to escape from the curse of death by His grace.

Now let us see from the Bible, who has brought the "Grace of God" to the sinful man for his Salvation?

"For the law was given through Moses but 'Grace and Truth' came through Jesus Christ! Amen. (John 1:17)

Further, let us go to another Scripture of the Bible, which says;

"Therefore since we are receiving a Kingdom which cannot be shaken, let us have 'Grace' by which we may serve God, acceptable with reverence and Godly fear." (Hebrews 12:28)

So, my brothers and sisters I call upon you to understand that "only by the grace of God" we can be saved, from the Judgement of God and also inherit Eternal life by the same grace. Amen.

Now, coming to the answer for the question of what is the primary requirement that God expects from the human beings is "Our Repentance Coupled with Faith" in the Lord Jesus Christ. Amen

Can anyone be saved without 'Repentance' for their sins?

Not at all! It is Impossible! Here is the Scripture from the Bible which says; "I tell you, No; but unless you repent, you will all likewise perish" (Luke 13:3-5)

Who has spoken these words?

Yes! The Lord Jesus Christ Himself, when He was in the flesh about two thousand years ago!

So, my dear brothers and sisters, Start repenting today for our sins as we are in the last days of the "Grace Period" appointed by God to escape from His wrath and judgement.

Now coming to explain the "Faith in the Lord", let us go to the Scripture of the Bible which says;

"But without faith it is impossible to please God, for he who comes to God must believe that He is and that He is the Rewarder of those who diligently seek Him. (Hebrews 11:6)

See my brothers and sisters, what a clear cut instruction from God! And 'Without Faith' no man can please Him! And it is impossible! He says.

If we could not please God, how then can we find the grace in His eyes? If we could not find grace in His eyes, how then can we be saved?

The Scripture says clearly that we must believe in God and that He is the Rewarder of those who seek Him diligently.

What does it mean?

It means that we should believe in God with all our heart and depend on Him for all our righteous needs of our life. Amen.

Let us go to another Scripture of the Bible about the "Faith" which says,

"Therefore, it is of faith that it might be according to grace, so that the promise

might be sure to all the seed, not only to those who are of the law, but also to those who are of the faith of Abraham who is the father of all." (Romans 4:16)

What do you understand from these Scripture of the Bible?

Well, if we follow only the law of God, we will be judged according to the law of God. And I am sure that not even one will be saved through this way, because there is no one who has not sinned against the law of God.

But if we "live by faith" and the same time not neglects the commandments of God, surely we will find "the grace of God" which will save us. Amen.

Let me take you to another important Scripture of the Bible which says about the faith;

"For in it, the righteousness of God is revealed from faith to faith"; As it is written, "The just shall live by Faith" (Romans 1:17)

What a wonderful Revelation!

The righteousness of God, which is essential to a man for the Salvation, is through faith in the Lord God Almighty! Praise the Lord!

See the Patriarch Abraham, the father of faith!, How he lived obeying the Lord God Almighty, even when he was asked to sacrifice his only son Isaac!

Abraham's faith in the Lord God, was demonstrated by his deeds, that is why the Lord God, credited to him for the righteousness!

So, let us live by faith, thereby righteousness of God will be credited to us like that of Abraham, after washing our sins in the righteous blood of Jesus Christ which was shed on the Cross for sinners like us.

Now coming to the last question that is what for we should be saved?

Well, my brothers and sisters, there are many answers to this question; we can put it this way that there are many explanations for what we should be saved at all?

To start with let us go to Scripture of the Bible in which the Lord God says

"I will ransom them (believers) from the power of the grave; I will redeem them from death!. Where 'O' death are your plagues? Where 'O' grave is your destruction?"(Hosea 13:14)

Yes! My brothers and sisters, to fulfil His promise given to the mankind, thousands of years before, the Lord God came in the name of Jesus Christ to redeem the man from the power of death and grave.

By His death on the Cross and resurrection to life on the 3rd day, He has granted forgiveness for our sins and further a hope that though we may die in Him, yet we will be raised to the everlasting life. Amen.

Then to punish the Lucifer that is Satan along with his thirty three (33) crores of demons (fallen angels) in the lake of fire, not only for their rebellion, but also causing the mankind to sin, against God and their destruction in the Hell.

Further, to reward the human beings, with eternal life who were, who are and who will be faithful to the Lord until the end of the earth.

Let me bring you a Scripture of the Bible concerning the eternal life;

"For the wages of sin is death; But the gift of God is eternal life in Christ Jesus our Lord" (Romans 6:23)

Now coming to the conclusion, my brothers and sisters who are in Christ, Hold on to your faith in the Lord Jesus Christ, who will guide and protect you by His Holy Spirit until the day of the Salvation.

Then to my brothers and sisters who are not in Christ Jesus, I urge you to find out who He is; surely He will reveal you by His Holy Spirit about Him.

Not only that when you accept Him as your Lord and Savior, you will also be saved by His grace and receive the eternal life as a gift from God.

Following Scripture of the Bible, promise you in this way

"But as many as received Him (Jesus Christ) to them He gave the right to become children of God, to those who believe in His name." (John 1:12)

"And the God of peace will crush Satan under your feet shortly. The grace of our Lord Jesus Christ be with you" Amen. (Romans 16:20)

So, I conclude here, calling every one of you to repent for your sins and in faith accept Jesus Christ as your Lord and Savior; then surely by His Grace, you will be saved and further rewarded with Eternal Life.

Allelujah! PRAISE THE LORD! Amen.

Printed in Great Britain
by Amazon

26011552R00101